BEYOND
CRUCIFIXION

BEYOND
CRUCIFIXION

MEDITATIONS ON SURVIVING SEXUAL ABUSE

BETH R. CRISP

DARTON·LONGMAN + TODD

Published in 2010 by
Darton, Longman and Todd Ltd
1 Spencer Court
140 – 142 Wandsworth High Street
London
SW18 4JJ

First published in 2010 by
Clouds of Magellan, Melbourne, Australia

ISBN 978-0-232-52843-5

A catalogue record for this book is available from the British Library.

Printed and Bound in Great Britain by
CPI Antony Rowe, Chippenham

For Meredith

Contents

Acknowledgements

Introduction

1. Taking up the Challenge—*Ash Wednesday*

2. Rejection—*Thursday after Ash Wednesday*

3. The scandalised church—*Friday after Ash Wednesday*

4. Conversion—*Saturday after Ash Wednesday*

5. Seduction—*Sunday Lent 1*

6. Too hard—*Monday Lent 1*

7. Fathers —*Tuesday Lent 1*

8. Steadfast spirit—*Wednesday Lent 1*

9. Suffering in silence—*Thursday Lent 1*

10. Confession—*Friday Lent 1*

11. Get real—*Saturday Lent 1*

12. Texts of terror—*Sunday Lent 2*

13. Low self esteem—*Monday Lent 2*

14. Wayward and bad—*Tuesday Lent 2*

15. Deliver me Lord—*Wednesday Lent 2*

16. Blessings—*Thursday Lent 2*

17. The favoured one—*Friday Lent 2*

18. Profound love—*Saturday Lent 2*

19. More texts of terror—*Sunday Lent 3*

20. Thirsting for God—*Monday Lent 3*

21. Impossible demands—*Tuesday Lent 3*

22. According to God's plan? —*Wednesday Lent 3*

23. Why doesn't a loving God prevent abuse? —*Thursday Lent 3*

24. Loving oneself—*Friday Lent 3*

25. The need for healing—*Saturday Lent 3*

26. Consequences of breaking the silence—*Sunday Lent 4*

27. Mosaics—*Monday Lent 4*

28. Spiritual direction—*Tuesday Lent 4*

29. Timeframes—*Wednesday Lent 4*

30. The need to be believed—*Thursday Lent 4*

31. The imperfect but loving God—*Friday Lent 4*

32. The long term effects of abuse—*Saturday Lent 4*

33. Survivors not victims—*Sunday Lent 5*

34. Put on trial—*Monday Lent 5*

35. Remembering to be thankful—*Tuesday Lent 5*

36. Miraculous survival—*Wednesday Lent 5*

37. No longer believe in God—*Thursday Lent 5*

38. A time for giving thanks—*Friday Lent 5*

39. This is the word of the Lord? —*Saturday Lent 5*

40. On a journey—*Palm Sunday/ Passion Sunday*

41. Anointing—*Monday Holy Week*

42. Betrayal—*Tuesday Holy Week*

43. Lord answer me—*Wednesday Holy Week*

44. Eucharist—*Maundy Thursday*

45. Crucifixion—*Good Friday*

46. Commitment—*Easter Vigil*

47. Resurrection—*Easter Sunday*

Notes

Works cited

Acknowledgements

THE FIVE ESSENTIAL FOOD GROUPS of the human soul are, arguably, love, grace, humour, friendship and forgiveness. I am grateful to the many individuals and communities who provided these gifts, sometimes to a stranger, during the year or so in which this book was written and over the many more years of journeying chronicled in the text.

In the mid 1990s, members of the Jesuit community at Newman College, University of Melbourne, first welcomed me to worship at a difficult time in my life. More recently, in 2005, they welcomed me into the Roman Catholic church on the Feast of St Ignatius. I am indebted to several current and former members of the Society of Jesus from the Australian and British provinces who have provided wise advice when belief in God was a struggle, modelled ways of living a Christian life with integrity, and enchanted my life with compassionate readings of the gospel. Australian Jesuits with whom I have discussed and debated matters of theology, spirituality and the church, and from whom I have learnt much, include Peter L'Estrange, Peter Steele, Richard Leonard, Robin Koning and Brian McCoy. Members of the British province to whom I am indebted include Damian Howard, Dominic Robinson, Philip Endean and Michael Kirwan. Alan Harrison provided much encouragement during the writing process, listening to many of the reflections which were written on retreat at St Beuno's in North Wales.

This book draws on and develops ideas that feature in a number of scholarly articles I have published over the past decade. I have been blessed to work with some very gifted editors who have nurtured my forays into the world of writing in the field of spirituality and encouraged me to believe I had projects worth pursuing, particularly John Honner, former editor of *Pacifica* in Australia, and Philip Endean former editor of *The Way* in England. While most of the prayers were written specifically for this collection, some had been written previously and earlier versions of some of these prayers have on occasion been shared with friends. Two of the prayers were included in an article previously published in *The Way*, and are reproduced here with permission.

This project has brought me back in contact with Gordon Thompson, Publisher and Director of Clouds of Magellan, whom I first met in the early 1980s when I was an undergraduate student. Without Gordon's enthusiasm and suggestions this project would not have eventuated in its current form.

Others whose support and encouragement on this journey of faith has been treasured include Michael Ross, Eira Clapton, Marita Munro, Meredith Wright, Raymond Perrier, Anna Abram and my friends from St Lukes Baptist Community in Melbourne. In Melbourne, I am also very grateful to many women who have shared their stories of sexual abuse and the complex impacts it has had on their lives. As we each sought in our own ways to move forward—and not let the seemingly overwhelming struggles crush our spirits—blessings have on many occasions replaced black holes of despair.

Those mentioned above are just some of the rag-tag army of friends and associates, located across the globe, who make my world a much richer place to be, even though the journey I have been travelling on in recent years is for many of them incomprehensible. Finally, as always, Mark Anderson provides much love, support, trust and respect, along with the spaces to write and pray, all of which enable me to live and love well.

Introduction

THE FORTY DAYS FROM ASH WEDNESDAY to Palm Sunday can seem a long journey, but the liturgical year rightly recognises that we need time to prepare ourselves for the Good Friday experience of Christ's crucifixion and the Easter Sunday of his resurrection. Almost all the prayers and reflections in this volume are anchored in the daily lectionary readings of the Roman Catholic Church. These readings provide both a structure for the book and stimulus to explore different issues from the perspective of a survivor of sexual abuse.

This book is the result of a journey over many years which began with a challenge one Ash Wednesday to move out of some long-ingrained patterns of being and thinking which were doing me no favours. Although coming to terms with sexual abuse and how to relate to God in the aftermath underpins most of the readings and reflections, many of the issues tackled here might equally apply to a wide range of difficult situations in which individuals find themselves

There will be some readers who can work through this volume, day by day over the forty-seven days from Ash Wednesday to Easter Sunday, contemplating the quote and the reading of the day, engaging with the reflection, and praying both the printed prayer and prayers of their own. But this book, which began as an essay aimed at pastoral workers and evolved into something perhaps more radical and unusual, more interrogative, will invite a range of readings. I suspect there will be many readers who will need to use the quotes, prayers and meditations at a pace and in a way that is more appropriate to them.

However readers choose to use this book, although it would be foolish to promise the joy of Easter Sunday by the end of this book, my prayer is they will have perhaps made a few more tentative steps towards this point.

Beth R. Crisp

Taking up the Challenge

Ash Wednesday

> For years, early morning was a time I dreaded. In the process of waking up, my mind would run with panic. All the worries of the previous day would still be with me, spinning around with old regrets as well as fears for the future. I don't know how or when the change came, but now when I emerge from the night, it is with more hope than fear. I try to get outside as early as possible so that I can look for signs of first light, the faint, muddy red of dawn.

—*Kathleen Norris*

Joel 2:12–18. *'Come back to me' says the Lord*

Several years ago I emerged from mass on the morning of Ash Wednesday and by chance met up with a friend. The conversation lasted only a few minutes but left me feeling devastated. Accepting my friend's challenge meant acknowledging that there was something seriously wrong in my life. Over the weeks, months and years that followed, I was lead to confront the reality of the dreadfulness of the abuse I had been subjected to, and the ways this had long impacted on me. I hope never again to experience such dark days as followed that Ash Wednesday. Yet I know that much good has emerged out of that devastation, like the bush that regenerates after devastating fires. Hence, each Ash Wednesday I give thanks for the then unimaginable wonderful ways in which I have been blessed and able to forge new beginnings.

Ash Wednesday has long been a time for Christians to take on new challenges for Lent. Often this has been in the form of giving up some pleasurable non-essential, such as chocolate or alcohol. However, increasingly, Lent is becoming known as a season for making new commitments to serve God and those around us. As I discovered, that challenge may mean committing to recognising and starting to address those issues within us which seek to destroy us, such as dealing with the consequences of sexual abuse.

The words from the Ash Wednesday liturgy, 'Repent, and believe in the gospel', are an invitation to take stock of our lives and once again make a deliberate decision to embrace the good news of the gospel. This doesn't necessarily mean having to do something massive or incredibly difficult. Perhaps it is just saying 'Yes' to God's invitation to live a little more abundantly in our current circumstances. As we read from the prophet Joel, this invitation is especially given to those of us who have been heartbroken and in need of tenderness and compassion.

> Gracious God
> In the face of reluctance and fear, help me accept your invitation to live more abundantly.
> It is not always easy for me to respond positively to such invitations, and even when I do, I fear opening myself to the risk of once more feeling heartbroken.
> I can only take up this invitation with your help—and you will need to remind me constantly of your promise of abundant life.
> Have patience with me when I seem to forget your offer.
> If you can handle these conditions, then we've got a deal.
> I'll check in with you again tomorrow.

REJECTION

Thursday after Ash Wednesday

> During the first few months after my assault, most of the aunts, uncles, cousins, and friends of the family notified by my parents almost immediately after the attack didn't phone, write, or even send a get well card. These are all caring, decent people who would have sent wishes for a speedy recovery if I'd had, say, an appendectomy. Their early lack of response was so striking that I wondered whether it was the result of self-protective denial, a reluctance to mention something so unspeakable, or a symptom of our society's widespread emotional illiteracy that prevents most people from conveying any feeling that can't be expressed in a Hallmark card.

—*Susan Brison*

Luke 9:21–25. *The Son of Man will be rejected*

THE EXPERIENCE OF SEXUAL ABUSE is too often the experience of rejection. Repeated rejection. It begins when the abusers deny our humanity and reject our unspoken expectations of being treated with love and respect. But what can hurt even more is the rejection from family and friends who can sometimes act as if nothing has happened.

This was the experience of Susan Brison after a rape and attempted murder saw her hospitalised for several days. Later Brison discovered that her family had been very concerned about her. But they lacked the words or the means to discuss rape and sexual assault. In Brison's case, some well-intentioned family members were convinced that acknowledging what had occurred would further upset her. Their perceptions as to what constituted care and concern for the individual felt to her like rejection.

Susan Brison discovered that her family did care very much for her. She was lucky. The reality for many survivors is that the revelation of sexual abuse leads to rejection or ostracism from family and friends. This is particularly an issue when the abuser is a family member or so-called 'friend of the family'. An implicit agreement for peace at any price is all too common among families bound together by their silence about sexual abuse. Individuals who expose the truth about abuse may not only be disbelieved, but ultimately rejected by family members. Having experienced abuse, they find it is *they* and not their abuser who is rejected by other family members. Among young people I've worked with as a social worker, sexual abuse by family members is often the reason they have ended up homeless.

Jesus himself was no stranger to rejection. His refusal to give up on the truth and be silent in public ultimately lead to his death. Today's reading from the gospel of Luke is an invitation to all of us who have known the bitter pain of rejection to recognise Jesus as our friend and ally.

> Jesus,
> You know what it feels like to be rejected
> by those who should have embraced you and cared for you.
> Be with me when this pain leaves me heartbroken.
> Stay forever and not just until I feel better.
> And when the time is right,
> help me show others that with your love,
> loneliness and rejection can give way
> to light and life.

THE SCANDALISED CHURCH

Friday after Ash Wednesday

I am sorry this has happened to you. The abuse should not have
happened. And it is despicable that you should have been ignored or
defamed for speaking up about it. You have done nothing wrong to
cause this and you were right to expect compassion and justice from
me/us. I'm sorry for all the pain, for all the times you shed tears of
grief, anger, disbelief, for all the times you doubted yourself, your
parents, your children.

I'm sorry for the way the churches' stuffups/ cover-ups have led to
many other things that can't be conveyed in a media bite, the unfair
and unbearable things. I'm sorry for the times even family and friend
failed to 'get it', distancing themselves from you all because those like
me with the power and responsibility didn't understand their job
description let alone the one thing their faith required of them: to
stand unequivocally with the victim/s and those still vulnerable, to
call the police, to counsel the perpetrator to tell the truth and make
sure someone visits him in jail.

I will do everything I can to bring my church to account.

—*Marilyn Born*

Isaiah 58:1–9. *What pleases God and what doesn't*

CHRISTIAN CHURCHES IN MANY COUNTRIES, and both catholic and
protestant, have in recent years found themselves embroiled in
allegations of sexual abuse. Reports in the secular and the religious press
of these allegations have been so numerous as to have become a constant

blur on the horizon. We have heard much about investigations, about the tragedies affecting individuals and communities, about financial settlements, and about clergy finally being ousted from pastoral roles. Although sexual abuse can occur in almost any social setting, the emphasis on scandal management by many church authorities has tended to obscure discussion of the needs of survivors of sexual abuse.

In 2002, Marilyn Born, an Australian woman who for many years has been involved in issues associated with sexual abuse by clergy, suggested an apology that could be spoken by church authorities to all those affected by clergy sexual abuse: an apology that 'archbishops or moderators or just humble parish clerics should be saying in public to all those children and their parents who have not been helped by going to the churches'. Many of us will never get any meaningful apology either from individual perpetrators or from the organisations to which they belonged, or still belong. Official apologies from churches are likely to be few and far between, especially when acknowledgement of sexual abuse has left churches open to expensive legal suits—to the point of bankruptcy in some dioceses. For some, the historic meeting in 2008 between Pope Benedict XVI and a number of American parishoners who had been sexually abused by Catholic clergy was an important step in acknowledging the devastating impact of sexual abuse and the need for apologies by institutions which have failed in their duty of care. For others, however, such apologies have come too late for the churches to retain any credibility.

Today's reading from Isaiah reminds us that those who profess themselves to be the people of God have for millennia been engaged in scandalous acts, and that God has demanded repentance of their scandalous behaviour. God demands no less of the church today, and we have been short-changed by churches which have cared more about managing scandals than caring for those who have endured sexual abuse.

God of Justice

We have been let down by churches which have proclaimed your word but acted without reference to your way:

When care was needed, abuse was provided.

When apologies were desperately needed, there were scandals to be managed.

When repentance was sought, we were sidelined or banished.

God of Justice

Grant us clarity to recognise:

That you never stopped caring for us,

And that our wellbeing was your highest priority,

Even when we were made to feel as if it were otherwise.

God of Justice

Help us this day to find you,

despite all the obstacles which the church has placed in our way.

CONVERSION

Saturday after Ash Wednesday

> In prayer, even more than in the other ways we deal with our experiences, we must be honest with ourselves. The familiar world around us and the even more familiar world inside us simply must be granted their full reality. We must face the fact that we wish we had the riches someone else has—and the fact that we wish the other would lose those riches ... Pleasure, pains, gnawing doubts, secret satisfactions or dissatisfactions about ourselves, difficulties or delights of any kind with ourselves and others must all be admitted. If we have come to that extraordinary world where otherness confronts us and we confront it, we must make ourselves ready for it in the only possible way we can do so—by offering it our own otherness.

> —*Ann Ulanov and Barry Ulanov*

Isaiah 9:9–14. *An invitation to abundance*

EASTER IS TRADITIONALLY THE TIME for people being received into the church, and throughout Lent there will be many people around the world preparing for this event. People often ask me how I of all people could choose to be received into the Catholic Church. I must admit that was a decision which took even me by surprise. After all, I'm a 21st century feminist scholar, and I sought to belong to a church which has a history of oppressing women, scholars and all who question church teachings, amongst its many downsides. Some who knew that sexual abuse had long been an issue for me were incredulous, with questions such as 'How could you join the organisation of the arch-abuser?'

There is a common assumption that sexual abuse almost inevitably leads a person to leave the Church and abandon belief in God, irrespective of whether the abuse happened in a church context. Certainly, sexual abuse has contributed to several people I know leaving the Church or having less involvement in organised religion. However, rarely told are the stories of those whose attempts to make sense of the experience of abuse have lead them on spiritual explorations, sometimes finding solace and support within a church.

I suspect my story is not so uncommon. Although churches are messy and far from perfect organisations, within them are many good people, men and women, whose presence in my life has been a gift. Through such people, I have been lucky enough to also find worshipping communities that offered me a place to nourish and sustain my faith without any strings attached.

In today's reading from Isaiah, God offers us a place of sustenance, arising out of the ruins. At a time when many churches are spiritually and morally in ruins, it is worth reminding ourselves God can make something new and wonderful from such inauspicious beginnings.

> Dear God
>
> It is a complex messy life which I can offer you. A life which is flawed, and a body and mind which bear the scars of memories too painful to speak. I am very aware of my imperfections. But often I marvel at the thought that this flawed being is precious and perfect to your eye.
>
> To my surprise, this complex and messy life has found sustenance and joy in a complex and messy church. While you offered me a place to nourish and sustain my faith, for a long time I was dubious as to whether this is what you wanted for me.

Thankyou that in this messy organisation there are places in which I can live and grow with integrity, and that this messy organisation can welcome someone whose life is as messy as mine.

I pray that your grace will continue to feature in my life, and hope that you will persist in guiding me as I enter a new stage in my journey with you.

5

SEDUCTION

Sunday Lent 1

> When I began to think about it, I realised that we all search for a
> viable life, and some of us search for a viable God within that life …
> It seems to me that to live life to the full is not just about meaning
> but about life which is sometimes lived with a passion in the face of
> the tough questions, the hard times, the setbacks and our ordinary
> human frailty. It is about heading into it all as though vivid and
> many-coloured life is possible, if we all hold on to each other. Some
> of us also take our God with us.

> —*Dorothy McRae-McMahon*

Genesis 2:7–9; 3:1–7. *Seduced into eating an apple*

SEXUAL ABUSE INVOLVES THE VIOLATION of persons who refuse to
consent to sexual contact, or who give consent only under duress, or
who cannot give proper consent due to immaturity, or impairment.
Sexual abuse can also arguably involve sexual activity where individuals
have consented, but without being in full knowledge of their situation.
There are numerous accounts of women who have sought counsel from
men, only to find themselves seduced into an 'affair' and who later
discover that they were perhaps one of a number of women in
concurrent relationships. These women may in time recognise that in
their vulnerability they were taken advantage of, that they were sexually
abused. While such sexual activity within such relationships does not
readily fit legal criteria of abuse, a lack of respect and absence of desire

that the relationship might enable the other party to flourish is another form of abuse.

Irrespective of what form our abuse has taken, we survivors of sexual abuse are frequently made to feel as if what happened to us was our fault. That can also easily be our response to Eve after she was tempted by the serpent in today's reading from Genesis. Yet in many ways the serpent treated her in a way similar to that which many perpetrators of sexual abuse treat those whom they abuse. The serpent found Eve's vulnerability and preyed on it, making it seem like she was making an informed choice, when nothing could be further from the truth.

In contemporary usage, the word seduction seems mostly to be associated with abusive acts. Yet seduction when not abusive, is a normal and healthy aspect of any romantic relationship. Similarly, when we feel as if under a spell while basking in the love of friends, we might also recognise seduction as underpinning that sense of being in loving rather than strictly functional relationships with others.

The writer of Jeremiah reminds us that seduction can indeed be a wonderful thing when he wrote 'Lord you have seduced me, and I have been seduced' (Jeremiah 20:7). After experiences of abuse, it can be too easy to become suspicious of the loving seduction which is on offer to us from God, and too easily rejected. Well after the physical injuries have healed, our inability to recognise the genuinely loving gestures of others in our life, including God, can all too easily become a perpetual legacy of abuse which we may not even realise.

> God of Wisdom
> I am not always as smart as I'd like to believe.
> Give me the wisdom in my relationships to discern between loving generosity and abuse.
> Help me to accept and not reject genuine love either from you or from others:
>> Love that desires only what is truly best for us; and

Love that does not impose false views as to what
that might be.
And when you think I am ready,
seduce me once again with your glorious love.

6

TOO HARD

Monday Lent 1

> I love going to church and being part of the service, but even when I'm asked to do a reading of something I don't because I feel unworthy. If they knew how I hate my father because of what he's done to me and my sisters then they'd realise I'm not good enough to be at church. Perhaps when my father's dead I'll tell someone.

—*'Geraldine'*

Leviticus 19:1–2, 11–18. *A difficult set of rules*

IT'S SOMEWHAT IRONIC THAT SURVIVORS of sexual abuse feel unworthy or highly immoral, rather than recognising that they are the ones who have been subjected to immoral acts. In the case of 'Geraldine' whose story is told above, the legacy of sexual abuse was that she felt not good enough to take up invitations to participate in her church, although it was something she would have liked to do.

I am thankful to have been part of churches which have not made my situation more difficult by well-meaning clergy or members of the congregation telling me how I *should* feel about my experiences. However, I've heard too many stories of people being told that if they want to participate in church, they must forgive their abuser immediately. Only then can 'healing' occur. Any refusal to comply with such demands can leave you open to accusations that you lack faith and are failing to be a 'proper' Christian, whatever that means.

If this has been their experience, texts like today's reading from Leviticus will probably cause difficulties for people like 'Geraldine'.

Rather than recognising all the laws which should protect her, the seeming impossibility of being able to forgive those who have sinned against her might be all that she remembers from such a reading. Faced with what feels like an impossible challenge, she is in turn too hard on herself.

Being a Christian is not an easy life choice, and for many of us is a constant struggle. While God sets the standards high, we would do well to remember that we are all sinners, and in need of God's grace. That doesn't make us unworthy in the sight of God. Despite our sins, God loves us and offers us forgiveness, even though we are likely to keep sinning.

Learning that God is not too hard on us, and does not want us to be too hard on ourselves may be the lessons we need to learn this day.

> God
> I really struggle to follow your commandments, but some are much more difficult than others.
> The one I find really too hard is that of forgiveness, particularly when it comes to loving those who abused me, and those who knew it was occurring but did nothing to stop it.
> If I can't love these people, am I a really terrible person?
> I know you understand how it is for me, and that you love and cherish me despite my shortcomings.
> Help me this day to experience that love and not shy away from it because of my ability to be too hard on myself.

FATHERS

Tuesday Lent 1

> When I was little I could never understand why God was supposed
> to be our loving Father and concerned with our own hopes and
> dreams when He didn't help me when I asked for the incest to stop.
> I never pray for myself now, because I realise that's selfish and that
> God doesn't want us to be selfish. I just wish someone would pray
> for me, though, because I do need help badly.

—'Helen'

Matthew 6:7–15. *The Lord's Prayer*

IT'S HARD TO EXPECT SURVIVORS to believe in an all powerful and all
loving God, if this God has failed to protect them from abuse from an
earthly father or father figure. Perpetrators of sexual abuse are often
known to those they abuse, and are often in trusted roles—family
members, clergy, teachers or club leaders. The dynamics of abuse within
family and church contexts tend to be similar, which is not surprising,
given that in the absence of blood relatives, the church acts in effect as
family for many individuals. Incestuous relationships between fathers
and daughters have much in common with sexually abusive
relationships between clergy and members of congregations. These
typically include the perpetrators having unequal power, authoritative
qualities and being in a role in which trust is usually considered intrinsic.
Hence, it may be difficult for survivors to respond positively to images
of God, which are associated with the abuser, or to trust in a loving
God. For example, 'Donna', abused as a child, and who as an adult

discovered other female family members who had been sexually abused, has commented that 'I just can't pray the Lord's Prayer anymore. I can't get past the connection in my mind between the word *father* and abusive sex. If I think of God the Father, I think of a man with a penis'. Or as 'Helen' another adult whose childhood was marred by abuse by her earthly father explains, she is now unable to pray for herself with the words that begin, 'Our Father in heaven ...'

> God my creator, whoever and wherever you are,
> you are amazing
> I want your vision of life to become the reality for people everywhere.
> Give me what I need today, and forgive my shortcomings
> Especially my inability to forgive those who hurt me.
> Lead me by example, and protect me from all harm.
> Thank you that this wonderful world you created was for us,
> to delight in forever.
> Amen.

STEADFAST SPIRIT

Wednesday Lent 1

The voice of lament is vital because it is more powerful than the voice of mourning. The voice of lament recalls the original creative word of God spoken at the dawn of time, to be the watchword for all creation. In the face of the loving, creative voice of God, the voice of lament acknowledges the brokenness of the present. The voice of lament is as primal as a child's need to cry. It is a way of bearing the unbearable. It is in essence supremely human, for it refuses to accept things the way they are. The voice of lament is not an end in itself, but is undergirded by the hope that God will act with mercy and compassion.

—Gill Goulding

Psalm 51:10–12. *Sustain me in this time of desperation*

THE AMERICAN NOVELIST ALICE SEBOLD once wrote 'When I was raped I lost my virginity and almost lost my life. I also discarded certain assumptions I held about how the world worked and about how safe I was'. Who we are and our relationships to others, including God, are tested in the light of terrible experiences, including sexual abuse. Sometimes this will lead people to walk away from relationships which they once considered to be foundational to their very being.

In some translations, one of the lines from today's psalm reads 'put a steadfast spirit within me'. We do not know what the experience of the psalmist was when these words were composed, but the words suggest a familiarity with feelings not dissimilar to those experienced by survivors of sexual abuse. But how we move from feeling vulnerable to a steadfast resoluteness, can be much less clear.

Gill Goulding suggests that rather than minimise feelings that may be intense and excruciating, the passionate outpourings of grief which characterise lament may be essential if we are to move towards a future where hope shines radiantly across the horizon. Although sometimes wrongly depicted as weakness, great strength is required to lament: great strength to lament that which should not have happened; great strength to name that which needs to be named. This is the first step to recognising past injustices and taking action to ensure that they do not occur again. This in turn is necessary if hope is to overcome despair, and for faith to become steadfast.

It is not just survivors of sexual assault who may feel they need permission to lament what has happened. Tragedies and disasters of all kinds leave us with the need to lament, but all too often we are encouraged to minimise the impacts of events on ourselves; we are encouraged to think of those 'worse off' who have a 'legitimate right' to their outpourings of grief and despair. While events that trigger lament can occur far away, for others lament is needed not for external events but for illness or injury which has resulted in a state of debilitation. My own experience has been that being able to lament experiences of abuse has been a crucial step in moving beyond a horrible past. It has not destroyed me and in fact has been foundational in fostering the development of a steadfast spirit within me.

> Steadfast creator, comforter and sustainer,
> give me the space to lament what has been and is no longer.
> Help me to see lament as something constructive, rather than a sign of weakness.
> Sustain me with encouragement, when it would be all too easy to give in to despair.

SUFFERING IN SILENCE

Thursday Lent 1

> Gentlemen, I wanted so desperately to be heard. I wanted someone to listen to me. I wanted someone to help me. I wanted to break the silence and despair that was killing me. I wanted someone to hear my story.

—*Craig Martin*

Matthew 7:7–12. *Ask and it shall be given to you*

JESUS' SUGGESTION THAT IF WE ASK, our needs will be attended to, runs counter to the experience of many survivors of sexual abuse. While we have not necessarily wanted to keep our experiences to ourselves, chances are that at some point we have found ourselves praying something along the lines of Queen Esther's ancient prayer 'Help me, who am alone and have no helper but you' (Esther 14: 3).

Terror can render individuals speechless, so that even if they desire to communicate what has happened to them, they may be physically unable to do so. Some may feel too embarrassed, while others may just want to forget what has happened. In some cases, survivors may be too terrified to speak of their experiences due to a perpetrator threatening their victims with death or violence should they ever reveal the truth.

The quote at the beginning of today's reflection comes from a statement to the US Conference of Bishops Conference in 2002 made by Craig Martin who spoke of being abused during his childhood by a priest known and trusted by his family. While addressing a specific context in which a culture of silence about sexual abuse was the norm,

Craig Martin's experience of wanting the silence broken is common to survivors of sexual abuse, no matter their gender, the age at which the abuse occurred, the method of abuse, or the social context. Yet given that discussion of even legitimate sexual expression between consenting persons is frequently a taboo subject, it is not surprising that a frustrating silence often descends to prevent any discussion or recognition that sexual abuse occurs.

> Listening God,
>
> Thank you for being everwilling to listen to my cries, especially when the words, which might explain my pain, are locked deep within.
>
> Remind me, whenever others denounce me for telling the truth, that to you I am a credible witness to some awful truths.
>
> Help me find others who, like you, will listen and support, rather than snub or silence me for talking about my experiences, so that there will come a time when I no longer have to cry 'Help me, who am alone and have no helper but you'.

Confession

Friday Lent 1

> Through all of this, I have remained a faithful and active Catholic laywoman. I have always sought to distinguish between the actions of one unfaithful minister and the Church but it has not always been easy … I have sought healing and peace in the sacraments, especially the Eucharist. Unfortunately, the abuse and its aftermath continues to make recourse to the sacrament of reconciliation very difficult for me.

> —*Paula Gonzales Rohrbacher*

Ezekiel 18:21–28. *Sinners will be forgiven*

TODAY'S READING FROM EZEKIEL is one of the many biblical texts which exhorts the people of God to renounce their sinful ways and choose a new way of life. This continues today with individuals in some Christian traditions being encouraged to confess their sins during Lent as part of their preparation for Easter. This can, but does not necessarily have to, be formalised in a sacrament of confession or reconciliation as it has become known in the Catholic Church.

One of the responses to a desire to develop a deeper relationship with God may be to want to confess our sins. But for many people this is difficult, including Paula Gonzales Rorhbacher, who is quoted above. While a teenager, she was sexually abused by a seminarian staying with her family for the summer, an act which has had numerous repercussions, for both her and other family members. As her perpetrator was not only trusted by her family but as a future priest held in esteem in the church community, Paula came to blame herself for what had happened.

There are few things as awful as believing we are too bad to be forgiven, but many survivors, like Paula, believe themselves to be terrible people who are unable to be forgiven. The challenge is to see ourselves as people who can be forgiven and to resist being unduly hard on ourselves when our imperfections seem apparent. In doing so, we may need to learn anew what are the sins for which we should seek forgiveness, and to distinguish these from those events when others have sinned against us.

For those times when I would rather cling to past hurts than acknowledge the good things in my life:
God of mercy, I seek your forgiveness.
Christ of mercy, give me strength to live as you did.
Spirit of mercy, sustain me when the way you call me seems just too hard.

For those times when I am too hard on myself:
God of mercy, I seek your forgiveness.
Christ of mercy, remind me of the times when you were gentle with yourself and allowed others to be gentle to you.
Spirit of mercy, breathe tenderly on me and help me to do the same.

For those times when I have had unrealistic expectations of others:
God of mercy, I seek your forgiveness.
Christ of mercy, teach me patience and graciousness.
Spirit of mercy, help me keep things in perspective.

For those times I have failed to recognise the genuine love and care which was offered to me:

God of mercy, I seek your forgiveness.

Christ of mercy, let me recognise your love in those around me.

Spirit of mercy, help me accept myself.

GET REAL

Saturday Lent 1

> In return for God's forgiveness, those who have been forgiven must
> forgive others. Christians pray, in the words of the Lord's Prayer,
> 'forgive us our sins as we forgive those who sin against us'. This
> principle has become a major problem for victims of abuse, who
> often find it impossible to forgive their abusers. The expectation that
> they must forgive their abusers if they expect God to forgive them, or
> if the abuser has expressed regret, when they are personally still
> unable to forgive, has added a layer of paralysing spiritual guilt to
> many abuse victims.

—Muriel Porter

Matthew 5:43–48. *Love your enemies and pray for those who persecute you*

WHEN I WAS A TEENAGER, the expression 'Get real' was a common
response to the seemingly unreasonable expectations that adult authority
figures imposed on us. Sometimes we said it aloud, but more often this
was a phrase we muttered inaudibly. As an adult, I've learnt that if my
objections to unreasonable suggestions are to have any chance of making
a difference, then a much more sophisticated articulation is required
than simply 'Get real'. However when really taken aback, the teenager's
retort of 'Get real' is about all I can muster. Today's reading, in which
we are urged to love our enemies and pray for those who persecute us,
can readily invoke such a response from me.

It wouldn't be so bad if in my prayer I could tell Jesus what I thought
of his command, perhaps wanting to add in some caveats for those

who've been subjected to cruelty and violence, and perhaps agreeing to disagree at least in the short-term. But this is the very sort of reading which seems to have magnetic properties, attracting moralising preachers and interfering busybodies who believe they are doing you a favour in reminding you of Jesus' injunction. Perhaps it's not surprising that many survivors of sexual abuse, when faced with readings like this one, struggle to believe that Christianity has anything sensible to offer them.

It is my hope, wherever this reading is discussed, that people would feel free to talk openly about how much of a struggle it is to follow this teaching of Jesus, and in speaking not feel afraid that they are being judged by others. It may be wishful thinking, but I'd like to believe that one day this might be possible.

> Jesus
> I want to tell you to 'Get real'.
> Don't you realise how impossibly difficult your expectations for us are?
> I don't know if I can ever truly love and forgive the person whose damaging actions have had such sustained impact on my life.
> And I'm not sure I would even want to, even if I could.
> So where does this leave us?
> Is there any point in me continuing trying to be a Christian?
> I await your considered, and hopefully compassionate, response.

TEXTS OF TERROR

Sunday Lent 2

> We know with our bodies, and we know the text and its infinite
> meanings when we become embodied beings in our own lived
> experience. Participating in the Apocalypse means saying no on
> many levels: no to this story as liberating for women; no to the
> violence of women's bodies; no to the sacrificial mass deaths. The
> stories of pain and violence and death and desire ironically locate us
> in the same ideology of oppression as the Apocalypse. The wayward
> woman is always quickly marginalized, mainstreamed, or massacred.
> What women readers of this text know with their bodies is the
> history of abuse and violence and death of the body of the female.

—*Tina Pippin*

Genesis 12:1–4. *Blessings for Abram*

MY BIBLE CONTAINS NUMEROUS STORIES and extracts which leave me
feeling noticeably uncomfortable in my mind, and sometimes in my
body also. Your bible no doubt contains the same text fragments as does
mine, and while there may be some texts which we may agree are
problematic, you might well be surprised by some of the texts to which I
have such strong negative reactions.

Today's reading from Genesis 12 is one of those readings that to
most people probably seems relatively innocuous in the grand scheme of
biblical texts. Indeed, on its own, it looks fine. What could possibly be
problematic about God offering abundant blessings to Abram, and the
subsequent texts in which these astonishing blessings indeed are given to

Abram, who becomes Abraham, one of the pillars of the faith for both Jews and Christians? The problem for me is when I read the stories of Abram/Abraham, his treatment of his wife's slave, Hagar, leaves me with no admiration for the man. With his wife seemingly unable to provide him with a son and heir, Abram gets Hagar pregnant. Some writers have suggested that this involved Hagar being raped. Whether or not this happened, the subsequent banishment of Hagar and her son Ishmael after the birth of Isaac was certainly not the kind of behaviour I want to see from one of the pillars of my faith.

Overall, the stories of Abram/ Abraham leave me feeling deeply troubled and perplexed. In an era in which many churches are finally adopting a zero tolerance approach to sexual abuse by clergy, the virtues of a man whose treatment of a woman which at best could be described somewhere between contempt and rape, are frequently proclaimed in churches to this day and we are encouraged to consider him an important role model.

> O God of seemingly endless wisdom, today you leave me perplexed.
>
> Why did you choose Abram to be a pillar of faith?
>
> Did you make a mistake, or is there something you are trying to teach me?
>
> Is it that you can use someone as flawed as Abram, perhaps someone like me, to do great things, or at least to make a difference to the world?
>
> Or is it that you give us blessings, despite our transgressions?
>
> I'd like to assume that you don't condone sexual abuse, even though sections of church hierarchies have seemingly done so for decades, but maybe I've got it wrong?

LOW SELF ESTEEM

Monday Lent 2

Of all the relationships in my life, one that has been among the most difficult is the relationship with myself; overcoming low self-confidence is an ongoing struggle. One might contend that self-denigration is a form of self-mutilation, and at times it has been a powerfully destructive force in my life. All too often low self-esteem has limited the opportunities available to me, and had an impact on the relationships with significant others in my life, including God.

—Beth Crisp

Daniel 9:4–10. *We have sinned and done wrong*

LIKE MANY SURVIVORS OF SEXUAL ABUSE, I fight a constant battle to not succumb to low self esteem. On a day-to-day basis, low self esteem can make it difficult to make any requests for assistance from others, even from those who are my friends. This includes making requests of God in prayer, whom I sometimes worry might consider even my fairly basic requests as being too decadent or frivolous.

Not only am I prone to developing negative self images, but I can easily start believing that others, including God, would consider me a terrible person. And when I do fail or do the wrong thing, even if it is something quite minor, I feel terrible for days. And if I don't watch it, I really do run the risk of fulfilling my beliefs as to how useless I am.

What I like about today's reading from the prophet Daniel is that it provides us with a model of how we can acknowledge our shortcomings to God but not be self-destructive. The people acknowledge their sins and hope God will show mercy and pardon them for all their wrongdoings. The more I read this passage, the more I see in it a people who can boldly confess their sins because they believe that God can forgive them, however terrible the things they have done.

Compassionate God

I would like to be straight with you about my shortcomings, but when it comes to it, I find myself reluctant to believe that you really will show mercy and pardon my sins.

Grant me the boldness I need this day, and everyday, to acknowledge my failings and to find the strength to move on, to make amends when I can, rather than let self-destructive tendencies take over.

In anticipation of increased boldness, I offer you thanks and praise.

Wayward and Bad

Tuesday Lent 2

> I could never confess my guilt, for I understood quite well that I was
> not to talk to the priest. I was a bad girl who could not be forgiven.
> All I could do was to cover up my badness from all the people
> around me. Even if I succeeded in convincing people that I was all
> right, I couldn't win in the end because God knew my blackness.

—*Carla van Raay*

Isaiah 1:10, 16–20. *Though your sins are scarlet, they shall be as white as snow*

CARLA VAN RAAY HAS WRITTEN of her childhood experience of being
sexually abused by her father who told her as a six-year-old not to tell the
priest at confession. Consequently, she came to believe she couldn't be
forgiven by God. No longer allowed to talk to the priest, and believing
that God was her friend no more, the young Carla prayed to Lucifer, the
devil, until she felt her prayers were answered.

Not only has the church at times condoned cruelty, it has conspired
with perpetrators to legitimate acts of violence and abuse committed on
its less powerful members. Through institutional practices, abused
women have come to see themselves as 'wanton', or as 'temptresses', as
unworthy or immoral. Films such as *The Magdalene Sisters* show how
the church in Ireland (and elsewhere) treated young women who were
raped with a regime designed to nail home the fact that they were
requiring harsh punishment to reform them.

Even if we don't consciously believe such a description about ourselves, parts of it have got in. We may well have encountered people who, once they heard of our abuse, would in no uncertain terms let us know that we must have been at fault. The names that women like myself have been called include 'harlot', 'wonton woman', 'scarlet woman' and 'temptress'. Even being called such names 'in jest' only reinforces the original acts of abuse.

On my fortieth birthday, I received a birthday card on which was written the words 'We are God's work of art, created in Christ Jesus to live the good life as from the beginning he had meant us to live it' (Ephesians 2: 10). These are very beautiful words in their own right, but were even more special because the sender knew just how low my self esteem was, and what a challenge he was setting me to accept these words for myself. Like God, he didn't see me as a 'scarlet woman' who was wayward and bad, but rather as someone in whom God could see the beautiful person I was meant to be able to see for myself.

> Creator of all that is beautiful,
>
> Challenge me to see myself as one of your superb creations, rather than as the wayward and bad creature I tend to see myself as.
>
> Rid me of negative self images, and replace them with the clear sight of your way of thinking.
>
> And help me to see in others, the beautiful beings you created and not the person full of faults which human eyes readily find.

DELIVER ME LORD

Wednesday Lent 2

When it gets to that point in the Mass (when we are preparing for the Communion) and we pray 'Lord, I am not worthy to receive you, but only say the word and I shall be healed', I always pray 'PLEASE God, heal me this time please!' but it hasn't happened yet. And so I know that deep inside, no matter what I do, I am still not worthy enough in God's eyes because of what happened all those years ago.

—*'Miriam'*

Psalm 31. *You have seen my afflictions and taken heed of my adversities*

PSALM 31 INCLUDES ONE OF the seemingly countless events in the biblical texts in which God has heard the cries of the people and saved them from their adversities. But when the legacy of sexual abuse continues for years, even decades, through nightmares, disordered thoughts and destructive behaviours, it can sometimes feel as if God will never hear my cries to be rid of this horrendous experience.

Over the years I have learnt that healing is rarely an instantaneous act, but something that unfolds slowly. Years of therapy have made a difference, but another great source of encouragement has been the many people who have shared with me fragments of their own stories of sexual abuse and the complex impacts it has had on their lives. As we have each sought in our own ways to move forward and not let the overwhelming struggles crush our spirits, blessings, and sometimes even laughter, have on many occasions replaced black holes of despair.

When I can, I like to go to mass on weekdays and not just on Sundays. Both the mass and the small worshipping community to which I belong offer me signs of hope and encouragement, which help me from falling too deeply into despair. And when I say the words, 'Lord, I am not worthy to receive you, but only say the word and I shall be healed', I remind myself once again, that this miracle continues to be enacted.

Healing God
what I'd really like is some instant miraculous healing,
But if that's not possible,
can you send me this day some signs of encouragement?
And some more tomorrow?
And the day after that?
And after that …?

16

BLESSINGS

Thursday Lent 2

> The systems of meaning that people build up are always fragile, for they are made up of the tiny fragments of their lived experience, the many loves, small and great, of their lives. Sexual abuse is a bulldozer gouging a road through this fragile ecosystem of love and meaning that a person has been painfully constructing.

—Geoffrey Robinson

Jeremiah 17:5–10. *Blessed are those who trust in the Lord*

BLESSINGS ARE USUALLY GOOD THINGS, something we can't have enough of, and it seems fitting that a loving God would want to bless the faithful. And it would seem fitting that as followers of Jesus we might want to offer blessings to others too. However, sometimes a blessing which is offered in a spirit of love may leave the recipient feeling uncomfortable, if not distressed. Why is this?

There is a priest I know, who would give me a formal blessing at the end of each conversation we had until I explained that this was an unhelpful dynamic. While intellectually I know that what was being offered was a loving gesture, it nevertheless felt like something imposed to which I had not been able to consent. In some strange way it put me in a situation of feeling as if control had been stripped from me, which was what the abuser had done many years before. We eventually came to an agreement that if I wanted a blessing I could ask, but otherwise he would refrain from something which was for him a natural part of his pastoral practice.

There were difficult lessons to be learnt from this and other situations where all that appeared to be happening was something quite innocuous, that is, the giving of a blessing. For me one lesson was the discovery of just how deep were the scars of abuse that had happened long ago, which raised questions of just how many other loving acts lavished on me had I rejected or had just gone unnoticed. I explained to my friend that his ability to listen to this sometimes troubled soul and to not turn me away was itself a profound blessing, even if it wasn't a blessing in his formulaic terms. That I also suspect was a lesson for him.

It was long after this incident over a blessing that I stumbled across the words of Bishop Geoffrey Robinson who had written 'sexual abuse is a bulldozer gouging a road through this fragile ecosystem of love'. It helped make sense of why I had reacted so strongly to a priest giving me a blessing and why, more generally, accepting love was so difficult for me.

> Loving God
> Thank you for all the blessings which you offer us, and for all those who offer blessings on your behalf.
> Keep holding us in your heart, when the scars of life leave us unable to accept the genuine blessings we are offered.
> Install in all those who love us, patience and perseverance to find ways of being blessing in our lives.
> And when you think I'm ready, teach me more about how I can bring blessings to my small corner of this world.

17

THE FAVOURED ONE

Friday Lent 2

This is our secret and you mustn't tell anybody. You are very special Sarah, very special indeed. Secrets can never be broken. However, if you do tell anyone, then God will know what you have done. Because I am a priest, God will inform me of your deed, and as a consequence you will need to be punished. I want you to remember Sarah, if God tells me you have been naughty, I will kill you. Do you understand? I will kill you.

—the words of her rapist as recalled by 'Sarah'

Genesis 37:3–28. *The favourite son and his jealous brothers*

BEING SINGLED OUT FOR SPECIAL FAVOURS can end up with disastrous consequences, as Joseph found out when his jealous brothers sought to despatch him from their lives. Similarly, many survivors of sexual abuse have good reason to wish that they had not been singled out for special treatment.

'Sarah' was 11 years old when her family went to stay with an Anglican vicar for a few days. Telling her parents that he wanted to give Sarah some religious instruction, he took her to his study where he raped her three times. Afterwards, with a nine-inch blade held to her throat she recalls him saying the words quoted above.

Having read or been told many stories of sexual abuse, Sarah's story is one of the most revolting I have ever heard. Rape by clergy, rape by so-called family friends, rape of children, and threats to kill if anyone is ever told are all dreadful in their own right, and each of which on its own is far too common. But what really revolts me about this story is the priest-perpetrator invoking the name of God to give him the right to kill her should she disclose what went on. I can't think of any other description for such an act as 'evil', a word I reserve for the most utterly vile acts.

That Sarah did go on to tell someone and that her story has been published is testament to her strength to defy such forces of evil. But she, and all others who have been singled out for abuse because they were special, will need our prayers for years, possibly for the rest of their lives.

God of love and protection

Today I pray for all people who have been subjected to acts of evil, especially those where the vileness of the actions is beyond what I can even begin to comprehend. Let them feel your all-embracing love, and let them know that they don't need to run the risk of allowing themselves to be special in order to receive it.

I wish this was just a few people I was praying for, but I know it's far too many for whom this is their lived experience. Some may even be people I know, and yet I'm unaware of their circumstances.

Caring for all these people is going to keep you really busy, but I know you can do it, and still be able to care for me.

18

PROFOUND LOVE

Saturday Lent 2

> … spiritual direction, worship and prayer are arenas in which the
> Christian experiences holy ground, a space of embrace in which the
> unconditional love of God is tangibly and personally felt, allowing
> the pray-er to experience her own self and its movements and desires
> as well. This provides the sheer novelty of a nonattacking other, a
> gaze that is profoundly loving rather than accusatory or punishing, a
> space for nascent self-awareness that evokes neither retaliation or
> dismissal by the other.

—*Lisa Dahill*

Luke 15:1–3, 11–32. *The prodigal son*

PROFOUND LOVE IS WHAT EVERY CHILD should expect from their
parents and other family members, but as a social worker I've seen too
much evidence of the opposite. We could debate whether this is because
the parent doesn't actually love their child, or is not capable of
demonstrating their love in a way that is clear to the child, or even
whether the child is too selfish to recognise the profound love offered
them. However, ultimately, these are just tangents from the point of
today's reading, which is that we all need to feel profoundly loved.

The church is another space in which we might expect to find the
experiences of profound love which we are seeking. Like families,
churches can stuff this up really badly, and streams of dejected persons,
leaving the church and walking away from any relationship with God,
never seem to dry up. But when the church gets it right, not only may

an individual feel profound love from those around them, but hopefully the profound love of God, which remains constant, while earthly companions come and go.

Finding God's profound love doesn't always come easily. I know I can be argumentative, angry, tetchy, or in other words not easy to be with. I haven't always been grateful to those who have loved me and acted as beacons for God's profound love, and have at times too readily rejected the love that was offered to me. Thankfully God doesn't give up easily on me, and nor have many others who are or have been part of my life. Without them and without coming to know what it means to feel profoundly loved, my life would be much poorer.

> O God, you are profound love.
> Thank you for your constancy in loving me, when I have been unable or unwilling to acknowledge this gift.
> Thank you also for the many others in my life who have loved me profoundly, even though I didn't make it easy for them.
> And if you can, enable me to become a beacon of your profound love among the people with whom I spend my days.

19

More texts of terror

Sunday Lent 3

> I try to tell my teacher at school. She says: You are subject to your father in all things. He is your lord as jesus is your lord. He would do no harm or wrong. He is right in all things. If you are punished or hurt it is for your own good. If he is too rough it is because he loves you. Pray to jesus for comfort.

—Elly Danica

Exodus 20:1–17. *Honour your father and mother*

IN A TOP TEN OF MOST DISLIKED TEXTS for survivors of sexual abuse, the call to honour one's father and mother, would probably come near the top of the list. As a child of about eight or nine years of age, Elly Danica tried to tell her school teacher that she was being sexually abused by her father, but was rebuffed. Unlike today's teachers who in many places are mandated by law to report any possible cases of abuse to child welfare authorities, young Elly encountered a teacher who not only thought her claims were preposterous, but that she should not even think of questioning her father's actions. What's more she was told, 'If you are punished or hurt it is for your own good. If he is too rough it is because he loves you.' Then came the final sting of being told to 'Pray to jesus for comfort'.

It is perhaps not surprising that Elly Danica, like countless other survivors of sexual abuse, ended up with mental health problems as she grew older. Being told that one must honour the person (or persons) who are abusing you, simply because they are your parents, is almost as cruel as the original abuse. And suggesting to a child that their troubles will be over if they pray to Jesus, is not only naïve, but suggests a huge defect in the judgement of the speaker.

Like many adults who have been abused by a family member, Elly Danica was only able to thrive by making a life away from her family of origin. Years later, this can invite further problems if outsiders who know nothing of one's past, start asking questions as to why one has little or no contact with other family members, particularly if they live close by. Again those who ask such questions have little understanding just how problematic some families are, and that to thrive, one has to keep the family at arm's length.

Jesus

What I like about you, is that you recognised the complexities in the lives of those you met, and didn't judge them by the rigid standards of your world. Show your compassion to all those for whom circumstance has rendered it impossible to honour their parents, or even remain a member of their families of origin.

I pray also today for all health workers, social workers, teachers and other professionals, who are required to report any allegations or suspicions of child abuse. Give them the courage to do what is right, to effectively and compassionately support the children in their care, especially in the face of opposition.

20

THIRSTING FOR GOD

Monday Lent 3

One client found it helpful to call what had happened to her 'soul rape'. Although her religious leader had not violently raped her, his emotional abuse—making her increasingly vulnerable to his advances and at the same time increasing her trust in him and identifying them as 'partners in ministry'—felt like the very rape of her soul. For her, the physical relationship, as emotionally damaging as it was, created less difficulty than the spiritual violation.

—Diane Garland

Psalm 42. *My soul thirsts for God*

AS OUR SOUL THIRSTS FOR GOD, we may find our lives taking a new path. At different stages in my life this has seen me participate more frequently in the liturgical life of the church. I have become more disciplined in taking time out of my day to pray quietly by myself, offering my assistance to various projects and groups, providing funds which were needed, among other things. All of these things are good in themselves and scarcely problematic. But it's not always like that.

Sometimes our thirsting for God is most acute at times in our lives of increased vulnerability. The church we might believe is a safer place for a vulnerable person than hanging out in a bar drowning away our sorrows. Indeed for many, including myself, appropriately friendly clergy have provided great support and encouragement when I've been grappling with life and seeking answers from God. While sometimes what they have had to say has been important, at other times, seeing someone who knew something of my anguish just smile at me and let me know I was valued was the encouragement I needed.

All this is as it should be, but as we've been made all too aware in recent years, there have been church workers, from right across the ecclesial spectrum, who have seduced vulnerable women while supposedly exercising their pastoral duties. Later they've often found out they were not 'special' but one of many who had been 'ministered' to in such a way. Variants of this would be the story of some women I know, who have not only given up on the church, but given up on Christianity too. And sometimes they have been joined in this exodus by family members and friends who have been appalled at what had happened.

So let us pray today, for all those who due to their vulnerability were not able to provide truly informed consent to enter into what ended up becoming an abusive relationship. And because the church is not the only organisation in which such behaviour has occurred, let us not restrict our prayers to those who have been taken advantage of by clergy or other church workers.

> While we should thirst for you always Lord, somehow it seems we do it more at those points when we are really vulnerable.
>
> When all goes well, we find what we need to revive and strengthen us on the road ahead, but vulnerable souls too often it seems, end up meeting up with those who would prey on their vulnerability and destroy them further.
>
> Where are you Lord when 'pastoral care' becomes 'soul rape'?
>
> For my friends it seems like you 'did a runner' and weren't there when they really needed you.
>
> Although I don't think that's true, I can understand why they feel that way and I don't know if you will ever be able to make things up with them.

Please keep caring for them, even though it will be a thankless task, at least from them, but I would very much appreciate knowing that you still love them unconditionally.

21

IMPOSSIBLE DEMANDS

Tuesday Lent 3

So what happens to the perfectionist who becomes a Christian? Unfortunately, this person tries his or her best to live the 'perfect' Christian life. This includes trying to win the approval of God and 'earn' one's own salvation. In my case, I believed I could never spend enough time in prayer or studying my bible for God to accept me as worthy. If I made a mistake, all my past failures were dragged back into the light, because surely I was not good enough for God to forgive. I would involve myself in endless 'ministry' tasks to pay penance (or so it seemed) for my sins, yet I was never perfect enough for God or anyone else.

—*Misti Joy Woolery Lincoln*

Daniel 3:35–43. *May our contrite souls be acceptable to you*

ACCEPTING MY LIMITATIONS AND IMPERFECTIONS is one of the most difficult lessons I have ever had to learn. Like many survivors of sexual abuse, I sought to rewrite the internal scripts which cast me as worthless, useless, dreadful, hopeless, etc, by trying very hard to be 'perfect'. In the past this has propelled me into cycles of frenetic activity and worry, putting impossible demands on myself, which has ultimately been as harmful as constantly attesting to how worthless I am. Not only have I compromised my health, but always being busy hasn't brought the desired happiness or contentment that I believed it would.

While others might argue that I still place myself under impossible demands, these days I am much gentler on myself. Like the people on whose behalf Azariah is praying in the Book of Daniel, I am far from perfect, and live in hope of God's abundant mercy for my shortcomings.

It's no use pretending I can write the perfect prayer of confession. Frankly there are some areas of my life which could do with improvement, and constructively recognising my sins and confessing them is something I find difficult. Yes, God, you already know the list is long and I don't have several weeks to write an itemised account.

But somehow, I don't think you are after a shopping list. Rather you seek an open heart and mind, and a commitment to live justly, lovingly and compassionately. It's not a long list but I wish it were easier.

Sometimes it's easier to come up with excuses such as I'm 'too tired', 'too sick', 'too hurt', 'too scared', 'too proud', 'too timid', than to be open to your calling.

So please keep prompting and prodding and refusing to accept my excuses, and gently open me to your love, even when I find it impossible to do the same for others.

22

ACCORDING TO GOD'S PLAN?

Wednesday Lent 3

> Another teenage survivor asked: If God had so much power and knew everything that was going to happen, why had He allowed her uncle to brutally rape her time and time again? Why hadn't God answered her prayers and made the abuse stop or made her parents stop drinking and using drugs long enough to see the abuse that was happening right in front of them?

—*Sandra Knauer*

Deuteronomy 4:1, 5–9. *Observe the laws and tell them to your children and your children's children*

GOD'S WAY, CODIFIED IN VARIOUS LAWS and commandments, is spelt out in a rather straightforward manner at a number of points in the biblical texts. Not only are we meant to keep the 'laws', but we are specifically instructed to pass them on to subsequent generations.

With a powerful God, and a clear set of instructions, this might seem to offer a way of protecting children against sexual abuse. Unfortunately, in situations of abuse, God's word and law are twisted. Hence you hear stories of adults telling children they are 'doing them a favour' by providing them with some 'practical education' about sex.

It must seem rather odd to children that God can proclaim strong laws that should protect them, but be unable to enforce them. It's a bit like living in a country in which the legal system has irretrievably broken down, and people end up doing what they want without fear of sanction.

Rather than believing God is powerless, a child may well be tempted to believe God is actually very cruel, and cares nothing about the welfare of children. On the basis of the evidence of their lives, this may seem a highly plausible explanation for what has happened to them.

Whether as parents, or as other family members, through our employment, or just as members of the wider community, we need to make it known that God doesn't tolerate the sexual abuse of children and nor do we. And if we ever find ourselves in a situation in which we need to act on behalf of vulnerable child, let's pray that we will have the strength required to do what must be done.

God of the vulnerable
I find myself disappointed in you. I'm not sure why you can create laws which should protect children from sexual abuse and then be so powerless to enforce them.

I can't believe that you could have been so naïve. Didn't you realise that people would ignore your laws, and that the laws alone would be insufficient protection from would-be abusers?

And what happens now? Can you use your powers to try and make amends to those who endure or have endured child sexual abuse? And can you increase your efforts to prevent abuse of our children, our children's children and in generations beyond that?

23

WHY DOESN'T A LOVING GOD PREVENT ABUSE?

Thursday Lent 3

These young survivors could not integrate the idea that God, as most organized religions portray Him, could really exist if He had let young children be used as sexual objects. One survivor recounted how she prayed to God to stop her father from raping her. She was furious that 'God' had *caused* her abuse to happen and to continue all thoughout her childhood and most of her adolescence.

—*Sandra Knauer*

Jeremiah 7:23–28. *They have not listened to me*

THE GOD OF JEREMIAH, SEEMS to be saying to the people that he will be their God, but only if they will listen to his voice. It seems the people chose an alternative to what God was offering. And so it seems, God is prepared to abandon the people, although never entirely, if at all, does he carry out this threat.

For survivors of sexual abuse, particularly those who experienced sustained abuse, the notion that God must have abandoned them and not listened to their pleas for help is completely understandable. What can you say in the circumstances? I'm not sure I would even want to argue as to whether or not 'God', in whatever form, exists with someone who has suffered so vilely. And I'm grateful that at times when I've grappled with how 'God' could let happen what happened to me, that there have been people who have been willing to have the sometimes long and difficult conversations in which I needed to acknowledge my anger, frustration and despair with God. At times I've even wanted an apology from God, for allowing the abuse to occur.

Had people tried to stifle my negative feelings towards God, I suspect I would have given up on God and Christianity long ago. And as for the young woman in the quote at the beginning of today's reflection, I'd like to think the fact that she was still willing to debate the existence of 'God', meant that she hadn't quite given up on 'God' altogether.

> God, whoever you are
>
> It's really hard to believe your PR people who present you as loving and caring, when you seem to do nothing about preventing abuse.
>
> Some might say that in standing by and allowing abuse to occur, you've breached some item or other in the Advertising Standards Code.
>
> So are you really a loving God? And if so, can you explain why I should believe this to be so?

24

Loving Oneself

Friday Lent 3

… the abuse victim needs to defy the abuser's consuming reality in order to claim space for herself. There is a whole universe within her, the uniquely created humanity God brought to life, which has been relentlessly attacked, often since childhood, and never had space to develop. To a greater or lesser extent, her very self has been suffocated. Such selflessness is not holy and not to be naively praised. It is a mark of chronic terror and suffering, and cries out for appropriate and courageous naming, remedy and healing, for the abundance of life intended for every person, every self. Authentic Christian ritual formation requires nothing less than this.

—Lisa Dahill

Mark 12:28–34. *Love your neighbour as you love yourself*

IN THE LAST FEW YEARS, I HAVE HAD colleagues who talk explicitly about the need for a healthy 'work-life balance'. Health in this case means not feeling guilty for prioritising family, friends and other interests, and avoiding the temptation to work nights and weekends on top of the standard working week. I don't find the balance easy, especially when I'm lucky enough to have a job in which I'm paid to do some of my favourite things and when many of my friends do related work. For me the boundary between work and leisure is blurred. And in a world where busyness is the rule, I find that loving others can be much easier than loving oneself.

For me, an important way of claiming space for myself has been to prioritise periods of time I can spend with God. A silent retreat of a few days, every now and then, takes me away from all the competing demands, with time to pray, read, think and just be. Not only is my relationship with God strengthened, but often my mind and body get a chance to recuperate from all the stresses and strains which I put upon them.

When not on retreat, which is most of the time, I try and mimic to some extent the intentional patterns of worship and prayer. Quite often I take a slight detour on my way to work and go to mass. I'm often amazed at how that twenty or so minutes not only meets my need for some time with God, but fortifies me for responding appropriately to the many people and requests for assistance which invariably come my way. Late in the day, I will try and snatch some more time for prayer, although I must admit that at times I'm not so successful at this. I reflect on my day, giving thanks and offering intercessions as appropriate.

Sometimes prayer is difficult and takes me into places I'd rather not go, and there are times when my routine feels more oppressive than liberating. At such times, I might pull back to a gentler regime, and when I can, seek out my spiritual director whose gentle encouragement and wisdom can be invaluable.

It has been a great surprise to me to discover how liberating prayer has been, and how when I pray regularly my soul feels far less suffocated. It's been a wonderful discovery, this important other aspect of loving my neighbour: loving myself.

> God of this evening and of every evening
> It is a tired body and overwrought mind which comes to you this day, and I have hardly any words left in me.
> Thank you for everything that brought a smile to my face or comfort to my soul, and for being there as a positive force in the complexities of all the issues and people I dealt with today.

Help me to love myself as you love me, so that my caring for others doesn't become yet another burden.

And now as I take my leave of this conversation, watch over me as I sleep and grant me all I need to live, and not just get through, tomorrow.

25

THE NEED FOR HEALING

Saturday Lent 3

> Awakening to the culture of silence, and, beyond that, to the human
> person as a broken unity, calls attention to an even deeper silence, the
> indwelling presence of One who comes to heal. This silence may very
> well be the starting point for creating a new awareness, a poetic-
> prophetic vision. Ultimately, such new awareness will be nurtured at
> the still point, where there is no avoiding the face and no denying the
> voice. For at the still point, there is only [Christ].

—*Rita Guare*

Hosea 6:1–6. *Let us return to the Lord who will heal us*

IN TODAY'S READING FROM HOSEA, it would seem that Ephraim and
Judah are rather fickle types who return to God regularly when they
need healing or restoring, but in between times go their own ways
ignoring, if not avoiding, God. In fact it seems quite normal behaviour
to want what is good when things aren't going well, and then lapse into
bad habits after a while. For many years I filled my life with noise, as if
to avoid having to confront my reality, should silence catch up with me.
Noise formed the protective barrier that also limited the extent to which
I allowed God and others to break through my defences so that healing
could occur. But then a change happened. The possibility of sitting in
silence for several minutes, before and after times of worship (an
impossibility in the protestant churches I had grown up in) was initially
one of the attractive features of the Roman Catholic world I had begun
moving in.

As I slowly found times and places where I could begin to explore silence, initially I could do so for only short periods of time. In allowing myself to enter into times of silence, I would want to limit the degree of discomfort I was experiencing as feelings of alienation, loneliness, anger and resentment surfaced. As I grew more accustomed to being in places in which silence was the accepted norm, some positive experiences began to emerge, and ultimately I was able to experience the incarnate Christ as a healing presence in my life.

Nowadays, I am often quite happy to spend hours, or even days, mostly in silence and actually get narky when I don't get enough silence and solitude.

> Jesus, you find us in the silence of our hearts.
> For so long I resisted you, because the road to you seemed all too painful.
> Thanks for your patience, in a journey of many short steps with lots of intermissions and times of turning back.
> But now I have found you and the deep consolation I was seeking, and I never want to give these up.

26

CONSEQUENCES OF BREAKING THE SILENCE

Sunday Lent 4

> The silencing of torture victims is akin to the cutting of affective links between the victim and others, a common experience left by the torturer's tools. Torture victims often experience severe difficulty in relating to others and lose those whose support they most desperately need. A great many victims experience, along with an inability to communicate, a loss of warmth and an aversion to intimacy.

—William Cavanaugh

Ephesians 5:8–14. *Expose the ways of darkness*

SYSTEMATIC SEXUAL ABUSE IS A FORM OF TORTURE. It promotes a culture of silencing that prevents those who have been abused from making contact with others—others with similar experiences, who could offer support and break open the isolation. Like many survivors, it was a matter of years, not hours, days or months, until I was first able to speak about what had happened to me, and then only in very select company where I knew I would be treated sympathetically.

What has been most surprising in telling friends about what happened to me is that many had guessed something horrific had happened, probably sexual abuse, and in telling them I was only confirming their suspicions. Apparently my secret wasn't as much of a secret as I'd thought. Most had guessed about my past from a combination of various mannerisms, responses and bits of my life history which they'd pieced together. And despite my fears, no one judged me on the basis of what had happened.

Today's reading from Ephesians encourages us to speak the truth, rather than remain silent because we are too ashamed or too embarrassed to speak. It's a lot easier said than done, particularly in respect of sexual abuse. It was only after meeting others who were able to speak out about their experiences that, over many years, I began to speak and write about my own experiences. In turn, I know that this has been helpful for others: for those who've been abused who have been able to understand a bit more as to how 'normal' their responses are; and also to those who haven't had such experiences and feel somewhat bewildered when anyone they know reveals they have been sexually abused.

Perhaps where I might disagree with Paul in the letter to the Ephesians, is that while it can be liberating to speak out, it becomes oppressive if forced to do so. Very few people know the full story of my own abuse. Partly because some of the details remain very painful, but also because most people don't need the details—knowing just that I have experienced abuse is sufficient detail for them to treat me with the care and sensitivity that may be required at some points.

> Spirit of Wisdom
> Thank you for providing me with some excellent role models from whom I have learnt how to speak out.
> Continue to guide me as to when and what I should say about my experiences, and discourage me from speaking out when it will do nothing but leave me feeling exposed and vulnerable.
> And when others need me to speak out on their behalf, help me to do so with the tact and sensitivity required.

27

MOSAICS

Monday Lent 4

> How is it possible to be shunted from place to place, to experience alienation and even abuse, and yet manage to emerge as a fully functioning person? In the case of artists, many have been compelled to search for spiritual answers because the very foundations of their lives were shaken by illnesses, broken relationships, dysfunctional families, and other traumatic experiences. But some of them manage to piece their lives together. How? Their creativity may be nurtured by hardship, but being able to pursue their art over a period of years requires discipline. The scattered bits of their self-image have to be put back together.

—Robert Wuthnow

Isaiah 65:17–21. *Creating new heavens and a new earth*

IT IS NOT UNCOMMON FOR PEOPLE to engage their creativity when trying to make sense of trauma. While for some this may involve them in arts and crafts, music, theatre, film, or writing, others turn their energy towards creative endeavours including building, home decoration, gardening or cooking. However we do it, it's our way of claiming something of that sense of new heavens and a new earth which the God of Isaiah is proclaiming.

I was particularly struck by the need to create something new and good as a way of 'moving on' from horrific life experiences when visiting a friend who creates mosaics. Both in her own life and through her work she has encountered horrific incidents of abuse of different forms, which have had terrible consequences in terms of her own health and wellbeing. Her creations include damaged remains of china and broken mirrors, and out of this brokenness she creates something new and beautiful. These are poignant reminders that the brokenness of crucifixion does not have to be the end of a life's story. And my friend's story is not an isolated one.

In many ways my own life feels like a mosaic. Somehow God manages to keep creating something new and wonderful from the jagged slivers of my own life, such that the whole gives off glimmers of perfection even though many of the constitutive components at times seem damaged beyond repair.

> Creator spirit,
>
> Take the broken fragments of my life, discard what you will and with the rest continue the process of transforming these disparate bits into something wonderful.
>
> I could try by myself, but you have a better creative eye for creating human mosaics, and without your touch there would be far more jagged bits.
>
> So keep casting your eye over me and continue creating, so that each day I will continue to be pleasantly surprised by the ingenuity of your artistic mind.

28

SPIRITUAL DIRECTION

Tuesday Lent 4

> When we find ourselves in a time of temptation or desolation, the director is meant to be a kind listener and a gentle support. The director should help to expose the ways in which the powers of evil attempt to block our ability to respond to God. The director reminds us that God continues to be at hand even at such times with the necessary grace of strength and light.

> —*David Fleming*

Ezekiel 47:1–12. *The angel brought me to the temple*

LIKE THE NARRATOR IN TODAY'S READING, we sometimes need to put ourself into the care of others and let them guide us, even if that's not our natural inclination. When, at one point in my adult life, several people I knew started seeing spiritual directors on a regular basis, my inkling was that this was not for me—I wasn't that 'holy', and besides I believed I was getting along just fine.

I finally relented after being told that if I was serious about wanting to learn more about Ignatian spirituality, then my reading could only take me so far and after that my learning needed to be more experiential and less intellectual. And the only way of doing that was to seek out the services of a spiritual director.

Over the years, and as I've moved from Australia to Scotland and back to Australia, I've seen a number of spiritual directors for varying periods of time. In some ways each has been unique, even though all have been trained in the same spiritual tradition. What all of them have done is to offer encouragement and wise counsel as to how I might find God in my life at that point in time. And at other times they've helped me see that God is very much in the matrix of my life, even when that was not apparent to me.

Spiritual direction is quite different from, and not a substitute for, counselling or psychotherapy. The role of the therapist is to help survivors reconstruct their lives, which typically requires engaging with the experience of being abused, often in minute detail. By contrast, the spiritual director is concerned with how an individual relates to God now and overcoming the blockages to developing this relationship.

As things have turned out, most of my spiritual directors have been male priests, although I am aware of many excellent directors who are neither male nor clerics. Despite acknowledging that their knowledge of sexual abuse was very limited, they have supported me in my explorations and offered some very wise insights in the process. As such, they have also been some of the men in my life who have demonstrated that violence and abuse is not inherent among males.

Effective spiritual directors are those who encourage people to explore the links between their lived experience and their understanding of God, rather than stifle discussion of experiences which they themselves are uncomfortable about.

Today's prayer was stimulated by a director's suggestion that I read the parable of the man who found a pearl of great value and sold all of his possessions so that he could purchase it (Matthew 14:45-46). It is an example of how prayer can take one into difficult and uncomfortable places, particularly with the realisation that one's images of God or of oneself are not what one would like them to be. I was obviously supposed to think that God considered me to be that pearl, but the accusatory voice of God asking Adam in the garden, 'who told you?' (Genesis 3:11) kept interrupting my contemplation. The subsequent discussion with the director brought further insights as to how I understood myself in relation to God.

God:

And who told you that you were not beautiful?

—that you are not a delight to behold?

—that you are not good enough for my love?

—that I would not put myself out for you?

—that you are not a pearl that I value highly?

Woman:

I can't recall who told me, but why shouldn't I have believed them?

Where were you when I was abused?

Where were you on the numerous occasions the world misunderstood me and treated me with disdain?

Where were you?

Where were you?

Where were you when the pain of life got too much?

God:

I love you and always have.

I am sorry that you have been so hurt, that you have not been able to see me.

Have I not sent many wonderful people into your life that have given you the love and care that you have cherished?

Have I not provided you with opportunities far beyond what most people can only dream of?

Have I not given you the very finest of gifts—intelligence, a loving heart, wisdom?

Woman:

But you let them damage me

—strip me of my confidence;

—try to make me feel I was always second best;

—make me feel that any act of kindness was not deserved.

God:

I would rather you ask for my forgiveness than do as so many of your peers have done and turn away from me. I can't promise you that you won't be hurt again, but I will keep loving you, and will keep sending people to you to reflect that love. Please trust me on this.

Woman:

My ability to trust was what the abusers violated, along with my mind and body.

God:

I will give you my hand. If it hurts too much to be touched, I will walk beside you. It's a long journey and I'm not planning on leaving you to make it alone.

Woman:

And I don't want to go without you. Please come and take my hand.

29

TIMEFRAMES

Wednesday Lent 4

God comes to us as a child comes to a mother, in the depth of her being, through a slow transformation of who she is. Anything else would be violence and violation. We are bodies, and bodies live in time. Just as it takes nine months for a pregnancy, so it takes time for broken bones to reknit, for fevers to be overcome. Healing and growth take time. We need patience because God comes to us not as an external agent, but in the very intimacy of our bodily being, which lives in time.

—Timothy Radcliffe

Isaiah 49:8–15. *In a time of favour I have answered you*

IN TODAY'S READING FROM ISAIAH, God assures the listener that she can always expect a timely response to her requests. The only problem here, is that God's view as to what is an appropriate timeframe is often quite different from what we might imagine it to be. At least that's my experience.

Often when I want something, I want it now, if I'm really honest. For example, when I'm ill, what I would really like is to wake up tomorrow completely well, even though the normal period of recovery might be days or weeks. And when there are unanswered questions for which there will be delays of weeks or longer for the answers to emerge, I can become quite impatient.

However, much as I hate to admit it, timeframes not of my choosing often turn out to be better than if they'd been left for me to determine.

For example, it takes time for most people to make sense of all the complexity and multidimensionality of the issues which can emerge when trying to deal with sexual abuse. For me, this was because there was only so much I could deal with at any one time and continue to function in other aspects of my life. Furthermore, if I tried to deal with things too quickly, the issues would at some future point return and I had to start the processing all over again.

We pray
    'Your kingdom come
    Your will be done
    On earth as it is in heaven'
And inside
The silent scream of my heart adds
    'In my timeframe Lord.
    Don't make me wait any longer
    than is absolutely necessary'.

I confess that often I don't have time for your agenda,
or even the agenda of anyone other than myself.
And I'm not always clear as to what my agenda is.

But somehow,
despite my lack of patience,
you,
dear God,
remain patient with me,
perhaps even a little too much at times!
And for this,
I must keep remembering to give thanks.

30

THE NEED TO BE BELIEVED

Telling women that they are the ones responsible for the violence directed at them or that they should endure their suffering as Jesus endured suffering on the cross is to make a mockery of the love of God for all people and of God's passion for justice, especially for the powerless and disregarded. Churches must be sure that they are not silencing victims so that victims get neither relief nor help from the community that is supposed to care for them. Christians are called by biblical mandate to stand up for and to care for those who are unable to care for themselves or who are the victims of society's injustices.

—*Youtha Hardman-Cromwell*

John 5:31–47. *A testimony that is valid*

LIKE MANY SURVIVORS OF SEXUAL ABUSE, Jesus knows what it is like to be someone whose testimony will not be considered valid on its own. He points the people towards the testimony of John, which, although he knows to be inferior to his own, will be more palatable to the people.

Relatively few cases of sexual abuse ever end up with a criminal conviction being recorded against the offender. Legal systems have often conspired to silence those who have been sexually abused and dissuade them from pressing charges against their assailant. Police and prosecutors have often been reluctant or unwilling to process allegations, except for those fitting into a fairly narrow set of parameters. Hence, many people I know haven't even considered seeking legal recourse for their abuse. If they've washed themselves, a very natural reaction to rape, then the remaining forensic evidence may be insufficient to secure a conviction. And even if there is forensic evidence still on their body, the very thought of further degradation from the whole legal process puts many people off reporting the crime. Women, in particular, have also learnt that should a case get to court, they might expect that their full sexual history will have to be divulged to the open court, irrespective of its relevance to the case. A complainant's mental health and fitness to testify may also be scrutinised by the court in efforts to discredit allegations of sexual abuse.

I know a number of people who have been vilified for speaking out about abuse they have been subjected to, and am grateful that those I have told have accepted, without a hint of doubt, my testimony about my experiences. Such acceptance has played a huge role in assisting me to make sense of what has happened, and helped me look forward to the future with a much more positive outlook.

> Jesus
>
> You know what it's like to not be believed because you didn't have tons of collateral evidence.
>
> Some of my friends have done it really hard, for speaking out about their experiences of sexual abuse, especially when the alleged offender was such a 'respectable' and 'respected' member of the community.
>
> Let them know that their testimony is utterly believable to you and to those who count in their lives.
>
> And remind all of us that in the ultimate court, you will accept our testimony that we did try to lead good and holy lives, despite great evidence which attests to us not achieving such ideals.

THE IMPERFECT BUT LOVING GOD

Friday Lent 4

> We come to church with our fragile identities, often constructed over against each other … We begin by invoking the Triune God, a home in which we may flourish and find happiness, liberated from the need to fight for our identity, to justify our existence, at ease in the uncompetitive and equal love of the Father and the Son, which is the Holy Spirit.

—*Timothy Radcliffe*

Psalm 34:15–22. *The Lord is near to the brokenhearted*

WE ARE ALL FRAGILE, though mostly we live much of our lives as if this were not so. In fact we probably need to live this way if we are to get on with the daily demands on us. But when something terrible happens, such as sexual abuse, we are confronted by our fragility and for a while may be utterly brokenhearted and inconsolable.

Today's psalm presents something of a paradox for such occasions. On the one hand, God wants to assure us that he is genuinely concerned for us, and that caring and supporting us is of utmost importance. There is a further promise that God will ensure those whose actions have been so injurious will be punished for their misdeeds. On the other hand, I find myself asking questions about why God wasn't able to protect me in the first place, and why so many perpetrators of sexual abuse seem to get away with their actions.

When I think about how many times I have wanted what is best for those I love, but have not done anything to facilitate this, I am confronted by my own imperfections. And if Jesus was both fully God and fully human, does this mean it is possible to have a triune God who has imperfections. That's a far cry from the God I was first introduced to as a child, whom I quickly learnt was apparently perfect and could do no wrong.

I guess I'd still like a God who is perfect, but perhaps my relationship with God will only succeed if I allow it to be like my relationships with those on this earth who I am closest to, who I have learnt to love, despite any imperfections I see in them.

I have on occasion heard the trinity referred to as 'Creator, Redeemer and Sustainer'. Together these three infect me with hope and courage to face the future, and above all to flourish. There won't ever be a time when I can say that the abuse never happened, but with the help of these three and countless others whom they have steered into my earthly life, a deep happiness frequently permeates my life. After living for years trying to manage the despair and sadness that are a constant threat to the brokenhearted, this never ceases to seem like a miracle.

> Creator, Redeemer and Sustainer—that's a pretty awesome set of attributes if you ask me!
>
> But I wanted more than you could give me. I wanted you to be perfect, or at least perfect as I envisage it.
>
> As I see it, a perfect God wouldn't let sexual abuse happen, or anything else that leads to us being brokenhearted and all too aware of our fragility.
>
> So you leave me with a choice—accept who you are with any limitations as I may perceive them, or not have you as part of my life.
>
> Knowing what you can offer me makes this decision straightforward and I want you in my life.

I don't want to live without that which you can offer me, because I want to flourish, and with you in my life that's a realistic proposition.

32

THE LONG TERM EFFECTS OF ABUSE

Saturday Lent 4

> It is often difficult for those who care for abuse survivors to understand the profound effects which the abuse has had. Survivors who are struggling with the effects of abuse years after it has ended are sometimes counselled by well-meaning friends or family members to 'let bygones be bygones' and live for the present. This is particularly a problem in churches, where a belief that Jesus has all the answers can lead to trite counsel from people who simply don't understand the questions.

—Patrick Parkinson

Jeremiah 11:18–20. *Unknowingly led to the slaughterhouse*

AT SOME POINT, MOST CHILDREN learn that the world is not a safe place, and that a degree of vigilance is required if we are to remain unharmed. As we get older, particularly if we are female, these warnings become more explicit as to how we can avoid being raped when away from home. We are warned not to walk alone, especially in dark places, not to wear clothing which is too 'provocative', not to accept lifts home from people we don't know, etc, etc. Yet despite all these warnings, people continue to be raped, even those who heed all the warnings. The reality is that much sexual abuse happens in contexts which are supposed to be safe havens, including one's own home and those of friends and other family members.

Rape is nevertheless always a shock when it does occur, despite a lifetime of warnings. Like Jeremiah, we had been warned of disaster but we nevertheless thought it would never happen to us. We too were often like the trusting lamb being led to the slaughterhouse, unaware of our fate until it was too late. And what has happened to us may have changed us so profoundly, that we are unable to simply get on with life as if it never happened.

Advice that one should get on with one's life and forget about the abuse and its impacts is unhelpful, even though it may have been well meant. However, this is often about suiting the needs of others who are unable, or don't want, to acknowledge the severity of what has happened, particularly if they think they might have been in a position to prevent the abuse occurring.

When traumatic events happen, some form of resolution is most likely to be achieved by those who are allowed to express the horror they have experienced, which may be for months and years after, rather than hours or days. Members of our family and churches may well be unwilling to stick around if they think this is taking an unreasonably long time. Thankfully the God of Jeremiah, and of ourselves, has infinite patience when it comes to dealing with our pain and commits himself to sticking by us.

> God of infinite patience
> I can't deal with those around me who want me to get on with my life and forget this horrible thing ever happened.
> Find me people who can appreciate what I've gone through and can understand why I'm reacting as I do.
> And if I ever get to the point where you think I'm ready to hear your answer, please explain to me just how it was that you didn't intervene and prevent me from being like a lamb led to slaughter.

33

Survivors not Victims

Sunday Lent 5

Western society is soured by a pervasive sense of victimhood. …
People even talk of 'the competition of victimhood': 'I am more of a
victim than you are'. This is not to deny that there are people who
are profoundly victimized, such as children sold for sexual
exploitation and women in many parts of the world. But the Church
can never accept that anyone is *just* a victim. Freedom begins when
people grasp the choices that they can make, even if they are
extremely limited, even if it is just to get up in the morning. If one
passively accepts victimhood then one dies.

—*Timothy Radcliffe*

Ezekiel 37:12–14. *I shall put my spirit in you, and you will live*

SEXUAL ABUSE IS BAD ENOUGH, but I really hate it when others try to
tell me how I should define myself in relation to this experience. For me,
the label of 'survivor' is infinitely preferable to that of 'victim', which
some people have told me I should adopt. While I appreciate that for
some people identifying as a victim enables the enormity of damage to
self and soul to be acknowledged (and allows for a refutation that the
person experiencing abuse was in any part to blame for what happened
to them), for me remaining a victim involves remaining hostage to a past
which frankly I would rather move on from. Being a survivor means
believing there is a future beyond abuse, albeit one that might have some
challenges.

Becoming a survivor can involve creating a narrative which incorporates the new self that emerges after dealing with horrific situations. While I have become a much stronger and more independent person, I can easily lapse into believing myself helpless and hopeless and am glad when friends suggest that I'm probably much stronger than I would imagine. One of the turning points, in moving from viewing myself as a victim to a survivor, was the realisation that the future doesn't have to be the same as the past. In other words, I have been open to the possibility for transformation, which has come in many wondrous but unexpected ways.

Today's reading from Ezekiel is full of this sense of expectation for an unexpectedly wonderful future. God promises to breathe his spirit into the people and literally bring them back to life. Although I didn't die when I was abused, it felt like something inside me shrivelled up and left me, leaving my often sad soul with the impression that I was little more than a corpse going through the motions of living. With a lot of love and care, as well as some very skilful therapy, I have been able to grasp the abundant life which had for so long eluded me. I have survived, and now I am thriving with the spirit of God breathing life into me.

> Breath of life
> Raise me from this malaise of the soul which leaves me feeling dead inside;
> Foster in me an identity which enables me to thrive, and even at times to breathe your spirit into those around me.
> And don't let me give up, especially when that is a tempting option.

34

PUT ON TRIAL

Monday Lent 5

> At first, being raped is something you simply don't talk about. Then it occurs to you that people whose houses are broken into or who are mugged in Central Park talk about it *all* the time. Rape is a much more serious crime. If it wasn't my fault, why am I supposed to be ashamed? If I'm not ashamed, if it wasn't 'personal', why look askance when I mention it?

—*Susan Estrich*

John 8:1–11. *If there is one who has sinned, let them throw the first stone*

WE DON'T KNOW WHY THE WOMAN in today's gospel was found committing adultery. We don't know if she had been married to someone whom she didn't love, but had been unable to resist familial pressure to enter into the marriage, and had now met someone she really did love and finally felt able to consent to a relationship, albeit one outside the prescribed norms. Or maybe she was a woman who had been deserted by her husband and entered into a new relationship which she hoped would provide her needs for both affection and for shelter. Another possibility is that she was being abused.

What does seem apparent was that while the woman was being called to account for having sex with a man who was not her husband, there was no such requirement for the man. This is the invidious position in which many women who are raped find themselves. Not enough to have been subjected to sex against their will, many women feel as if others are condemning them, as if it were they who were guilty of an offence. Not surprisingly, most women I know who have been raped have spent years talking of their experiences only to those whom they trusted would not judge them. Having established that speaking about the crimes committed on our bodies was not necessarily going to lead to condemnation, some of us have gained more confidence to speak or write about being survivors of sexual abuse in wider contexts. But this is rarely without some trepidation as to who might want to throw 'stones' at us or show their condemnation in some other way.

This desire to avoid stoning can also have the effect of us being unable to find ways of coming to terms with our own shortcomings that are not destructive. The trials which we subject ourselves to can be even more fierce than those which the wider world may bring our way.

> This is the prayer of confession of someone who tries to live lovingly and graciously but does not always succeed.
>
> This is the prayer of confession of someone who has been hurt and who at times has found it easier to be stuck in the hurt than recognise the web of love gradually being woven by those who have befriended her.
>
> This is the prayer of confession of someone who would like to love God more, but doesn't always find it easy or straightforward.
>
> And this is the prayer of confession of someone who is sometimes unsure of where God is leading her, or even if God is leading her, despite all the evidence to the contrary.

35

Remembering to be thankful

Tuesday Lent 5

The human soul hungers for sustenance, nurturance, inspiration, for connection to something greater than itself. It glorifies the divine, the holy, and finds rapture in its presence. For some, this hunger is fed by the glories of nature. The sight of the sun setting, the sound of roaring ocean waves, the sweet seduction of a gentle breeze connects us to something grand and glorious. For some this hunger is fed by the rituals and traditions of a religion or self-help network. For others it is fed by loving relationships. For some, it is not fed at all.

—*Rachel Lev*

Psalm 102:16–22. *God will provide for our needs*

FINDING THE THINGS WHICH NURTURE our souls and for which we can be thankful is frequently a challenge. For those of us who gain much nurture from our friends and the communities of which we are a part, the challenge comes as the circumstances of our lives change and evolve. Taking up new opportunities may leave us far from the individuals and communities that have sustained us. But even if we don't move, in an era in which transience is the norm for many, those who have welcomed us into their lives may have gone somewhere else and be much less present to us.

That there are people in the world who treat me as if I am precious has been a balm which has soothed the pains of abuse. Hence, when I find myself, for whatever reason, unable to spend time regularly with much loved friends, it is easy to become despondent and not see the many wonderful things, which could leave me feeling thankful.

Whatever else is happening, and however imperfect that might seem to be, I find it is important to take time each day to recall the ways in which God does provide for me everyday, especially when I'm not feeling like there's much to be thankful for.

> Because good things happen.
> Because good people seep into my life.
> Because.
> Because.
> Because of all that is good in my life, which can be easily forgotten when bad things happen.
> Because of all this and more.
> I give thanks.

36

Miraculous Survival

Wednesday Lent 5

The effects of sexual exploitation are worse than a middle ear infection that takes a long time to heal and leaves scar tissue that never heals. It is more difficult than having 30 shock treatments decreed by a Turkish intern when one is only 17 year and under the auspices of alcoholic and abusive parents. Recovery from sexual exploitation is harder than recovery from 17 years of substance abuse. Sexual exploitation is more painful than being the last person your friend talks to before she jumps off the Windsor Bridge.

—Laurel Lewis

Daniel 3:14–28. *Surviving a seemingly certain death*

WHAT OFTEN SURPRISES ME IS not how badly sexual abuse has impacted on some people's lives, but rather how remarkably unscathed many people seem after enduring unspeakably bad abuse. Of course, I know that, unlike Shadrach, Meshach and Abednego who emerged unscathed from a fiery furnace, most survivors of sexual abuse have some evidence of wounding of body, mind and soul.

I have no doubt that Shadrach, Meshach and Abednego were men of great faith and integrity and that God did rescue them from a certain death. However, we shouldn't be persuaded, either by ourselves or by others, that we have any less faith than these three, because we did not survive our ordeals unscathed. Although it sometimes seems so, life is not a competition to see who can survive the most horrendous ordeal and remain least harmed. Nor is the amount of damage received related to how much God loves us.

Instead, this is a story which encourages us to continue believing in God, no matter how much more attractive worshipping other idols might seem. We have experienced events much more horrendous than many people could readily imagine and we have survived. As such, despite our wounds, like Shadrach, Meshach and Abednego, our lives also bear witness to a God who can work miracles.

God of the scathed and unscathed

Help us to see beyond our wounds and marvel at the extent of our healing.

Challenge us whenever we take the bait and start accepting that our wounds are evidence that we are less loved or less faithful than Shadrach, Meshach and Abednego.

Encourage us when we would rather not continue enduring our pain and seek comfort from other idols.

And when we really need it, send us an angel.

37

NO LONGER BELIEVE IN GOD

Thursday Lent 5

We bear witness in part by listening to survivor stories. Then we address the questions: How do we help people heal? What do we do to stop these abuses? Where do we start? Simple answers will not work. Blaming and shaming won't work even though they're tempting. Healing and prevention happen together when we listen to the stories that must be told, then share resources and a commitment to peaceful relationships. Healing comes when we 'shine the light' on what is, what was, and what needs to be.

—Rachel Lev

John 8:51–59. *The dangers in telling one's story*

IF THE INITIAL EXPERIENCE OF SEXUAL ABUSE itself hasn't lead to survivors ditching any belief in God, then attempting to speak out about one's experiences can have the same effect. After being called a liar and subjected to other forms of violence for telling one's story, it's understandable that many survivors no longer feel they can believe in God. Even for those who maintain some degree of faith, it is often a struggle to believe in the Christian God, and in a Jesus who we are told died for our sins.

What interests me in today's gospel is that clearly Jesus knew what it felt like to be treated hideously for telling his story. Having told his story of having preceded Abraham, the crowds became hostile and called him a liar. They then attempted to physically harm him, and the story ends with Jesus fleeing for his own safety.

I don't know what Jesus prayed after this encounter in the temple, but if he was fully human as we are told he was, he may well have talked to God about his struggles and disillusionment, of finding his task on earth to be unreasonable, and wanting to be somewhere more comfortable.

Gracious and loving God ...

That much I want to believe, even if sometimes it's a struggle.

You know my confusion and disillusionment,

Of feeling lost and alienated,

Of expectations not realised,

Of not being sure about lots of things.

In my pain and confusion.

Heal me of the hurts which hinder me from fully appreciating all the gifts that you offer me, and

Give me the faith to keep going when I'd rather not.

These are big asks

But am I unreasonable when you ask so much of me?

As Easter approaches, I look forward to the joy of renewing my baptismal vows,

And I know you will be with me,

Even though I might prefer to be somewhere else.

38

A TIME FOR GIVING THANKS

Friday Lent 5

... I entered a period of my life that I recognized to be dark: a phase of rebellion where I was testing out the boundaries ... Much of what I did during that phase was fairly trivial, but I was very young and could feel the weight of it on my conscience. Soon I was longing for the recovery of innocence and wholesomeness again. It has always been in my personality to have strong moral conscience, but also to be prone to black moods and outbursts. Ever since, there has been a battle within to integrate this seemingly conflicting rebellious streak with a side of me that hungers and thirsts for righteousness.

At that time I had the first of what was to become a recurring experience which I would later recognize as grace trying to break through into my life. I felt a sense of the sacred by virtue of distance and the comparison of light with dark.

—Joanna Gilbert

Jeremiah 20:10–13. *The God who stands by us*

AFTER BAD THINGS HAVE HAPPENED, it is easy to become bitter and feel sorry for ourselves. Some of us aren't always easy be around even at the best of times, but when anger is seething in us it is only the courageous or foolhardy who will voluntarily spend their time with us.

As Jeremiah reminds us in today's reading, even after lots of things have gone wrong, there are still things to give thanks for. Maybe we're like Jeremiah and are able to sing praises in thanks to God for surviving a period of adversity. Yet I must admit sometimes I don't feel an iota of thankfulness in my body, and feeling thankful is something I have to work hard at.

Whether or not I'm in a space where I'm genuinely able to feel thankful to God for where I'm at, there are many people and events in my life for whom I am truly appreciative. In particular, I'm grateful for those who have stuck by me when in my anger and pain I've lashed out at those in close proximity who were often those who least deserved such treatment from me. They have taught me so much what loving and caring for another involves, and that I deserve nothing less than the love and respect which they offer me. As such their presence in my life has been nothing short of a marvellous gift.

> For those who encounter our troubled souls
> but continue to see potential in us
>> God, we give thanks.

> For those who have the courage to lovingly confront
> when we run off the rails
>> God, we give thanks.

> For those who forgive
> and help us to learn that we can be forgiven
>> God, we give thanks.

> For those whose presence in our life is gift
> even when we don't know it
>> God, we give thanks.

THIS IS THE WORD OF THE LORD?

Saturday Lent 5

> She was asked to preach in chapel during Rape Crisis Week. She had
> never heard a sermon about rape and had no idea how to preach one.
> So she simply stood in the pulpit and read stories from the Bible,
> stories about sexual violence. There were too many to read them all.
> When the service was over one of her colleagues said, 'I don't like
> getting hit over the head with this kind of stuff. You're preaching to
> the wrong crowd. That kind of thing doesn't happen here.'
> All week long, students, women and men, came by her office to tell
> their own stories of violation.

> *—Danna Nolan Fewell*

Ezekiel 37:21–28. *No longer shall they defile themselves says the Lord*

WHEN MAKING THEIR SELECTIONS OF readings, producers of
lectionaries typically have far more material at their hands than they can
utilise, particularly from the Old Testament, even when selecting
readings for every Sunday for a three or four year period. The numerous
stories of rape and sexual abuse tend to remain in the discard pile.
Hence, the Christian who primarily relies on hearing the word of God
pronounced each week in church can easily be very surprised if the
standard readings are altered or if they spend some time reading
unfamiliar parts of Scripture to themselves.

Nevertheless, a lack of piety among the people of Israel is readily
apparent if we listen or read closely today's reading from Ezekiel. While
the writer of this text is not explicit as to the sins of the people, the

gravity of their actions is such that one may well imagine that their sins included some form of sexual abuse. What's more, while we in the pews may not want to acknowledge that such things happen in our midst, the God of Ezekiel is clearly aware of what has been going on and wants nothing less than a total transformation of the Israelites.

In many churches, the promulgation of scriptural readings from texts other than the gospels concludes with the reader announcing, 'This is the word of the Lord'. I must admit that sometimes when it comes to this pronouncement, I'm not at all sure that I want to assent to such a claim by responding, 'Thanks be to God'. But while I might find some biblical stories distasteful, I am glad to know that the stories of rape have been preserved down through the millennia. While churches may have avoided preaching about rape from the pulpit, the biblical texts have provided much needed evidence to many women that they are not alone in their experiences.

> I hear the words 'This is the word of the lord' and something within thinks this should have been asked as a question.
> It was bad enough to have my lack of consent ignored by the abuser, but being asked to assent to something I cannot agree with is pretty tough also.
> So next time you hear me mouth the words 'Thanks be to God', but not really mean it, consider that I've decided to take it as a question on notice: 'This is the word of the Lord?'
> And encourage me, prodding when necessary, to take some time to see how I can find you in pieces of scripture in which to me you're not readily apparent.

40

ON A JOURNEY

Palm Sunday/ Passion Sunday

Choices are difficult. There are always places where the road divides, and we have to choose one path or another. The crossroads are challenging places, whether the crossing involves starting a new job, beginning a relationship, or trying a religious vocation. Wherever our journey might take us, I am convinced that we are *summoned* to begin: we do not simply look around, decide and then walk forward unaided. Something about the path must first catch our eye. More often than not, we act without anything like full knowledge of what we will be letting ourselves in for. Looking back, we sometimes feel that if we had known, we might not have begun at all. What is it we see to encourage us into making such a remarkable leap?

—*Mark Barrett*

Luke 19:28–40. *The journey to Jerusalem*

IT'S NOT CLEAR JUST WHY JESUS felt the need to go to Jerusalem during the festival. However in many cities festivals attract large crowds of onlookers, and, if the organisers are any good, a bevy of celebrities as well. While there is no evidence of Jesus being an invited celebrity, the crowds treated him as if he was. As to how much Jesus knew of his fate, of his impending death and resurrection is also unclear. In the gospels of Matthew and John, the story of Jesus' processing into Jerusalem is accompanied by suggestions that some aspects of the journey were to fulfil prophecies, but in Mark and Luke such suggestions are not explicit.

From what we do know about Jesus, it's likely that his decision to go to Jerusalem was intentional, and there may well have been other options available to him, such as visiting his friends at Bethany. He also had a habit of making decisions based on what he believed was right for him, and not necessarily taking the easy option.

Survivors of sexual abuse have often had to negotiate a path interrupted by difficult choices. When is it safe to unlock the secrets within us? Who does one tell and how much does one tell about what one has experienced? Who can be trusted to respect us and our stories and understand our need for some aspects of our story to remain untold? Are we going to seek legal redress or press charges against the perpetrators? None of these questions are easily answered and they differ for each person. Furthermore, some actions, like revealing information about one's abuse, can never be undone, so careful discernment is necessary to ensure we don't land ourselves in an even more difficult situation. Yet there will be times when we are beckoned to take a leap, not fully knowing what comes next, and on occasion making that choice to step into the unknown may be the best thing we can do.

> All-knowing God
>> You understand everything about me,
>> much more than anyone else in my life.
>> What's more, you can be trusted not to blab
>> about this horrid secret which mostly remains locked
>> within.

> Wise counsellor
>> Help me to discern what I can say and to whom,
>> so I can unload this terrible burden of keeping silent
>> about what happened to me.

41

Anointing

Monday Holy Week

I'm sorry. I don't mean to be hurtful or dangerous. I want to be a gentle creature, a kind soul, a gift. But his abuse left me believing I am evil and deeply flawed, empty and frightened. So I beseech you to be careful before you touch my jagged edges—before you reach out to hold me because if you take me on your lap I may cut you off at the knees before either one of us knows what has happened and then we will both be sorry.

—Rachel Lev

John 12:1–11. *An anointing and a controversy*

WHEN WE GREET SOMEONE WITH whom we share some affection, it is not uncommon for us to touch each other. Depending on circumstances, norms and our own preferences, in public the ways this might occur include kissing, hugging or holding hands. In Jesus' time, welcoming a guest properly could extend to washing their feet, not just in everyday soap and water but using the finest scented oils. As an adult, there are very few occasions when I've had my feet washed by others, and most of these would have occurred in Maundy Thursday masses, but even then it can be a luxurious experience.

When Mary washed Jesus' feet, she did so using an expensive perfume, which raised the ire of Judas Iscariot who felt the money would have been better used to provide for the poor. While Judas and Jesus argued about whether the cost of one jar of perfume could really change the fortunes of the world's poor, the point that needs to be remembered is that Mary did something which cost her dearly. Not only had it cost her a substantial sum of money, but in the eyes of some, she had also put her reputation at risk in caring for Jesus in this way.

Whereas the cost of giving is often highlighted, the cost of letting someone touch us results in often unmentioned levels of heightened anxiety for many survivors of sexual abuse. We know how it feels to have our bodies violated and in our heightened vigilance to avoid that happening again, we can become wary of all physical contact. In the course of a developing friendship, a kiss or hug may be a wondrous gift, but if people force these onto me too early in a relationship for me to feel safe, I will sometimes back away. Like Rachel Lev in the above quote, in a split second an offer of affection can be misinterpreted leaving both parties feeling hurt and confused. On occasion, this has seen potential friendships disappear before they really even got going. However, sometimes, when I've been able to explain my reticence to overly demonstrative displays of affection and that there are reasons why it can take me a while to be able to reciprocate offers of physical affection, fledgling friendships have deepened. And from those who've held back until I was ready, the physical affection they now offer is truly a gift.

> To the God who stands by us in the midst of controversies, especially those arising from the generosity of friends or would-be friends:
>
> Help me to discern the correct response in each new situation, and not just automatically default to a position of reticence when offered a sign of affection.
>
> Teach me through those I can trust, that physical touch mostly doesn't mean feeling violated and when lovingly offered can be deeply healing.

91

And when I screw things up, and not only I'm feeling hurt but others also, send your love and wisdom into the situation.

42

BETRAYAL

Tuesday Holy Week

> Sexual abuse of minors by a significant number of priests and religious, together with the attempts by many church authorities to conceal the abuse, constitute one of the ugliest stories ever to emerge from the Catholic Church. It is hard to imagine a more total contradiction of everything Jesus Christ stood for, and it would be difficult to overestimate the pervasive and lasting harm it has done to the Church.

—Geoffrey Robinson

John 13:21–38. *Jesus and his betrayer*

THE BETRAYAL OF JESUS BY PETER raises the question: How could Peter do such a thing to someone whom he claimed to love as much as anyone could love someone else? Similar questions emerge from many survivors of sexual abuse, especially those who have been abused by someone who claims to love and care for them.

Today's quote is from Geoffrey Robinson, who was a bishop in the Catholic Church. While Robinson was specifically writing about abuse which occurred within his church, the deletion of a few words from this quote results in a statement that encapsulates the experience of betrayal, so common amongst those of us who have been sexually abused:

> Sexual abuse … together with the attempts … to conceal the abuse, constitute one of the ugliest stories ever to emerge … It is hard to imagine a more total contradiction of everything Jesus Christ stood

for, and it would be difficult to overestimate the pervasive and lasting harm it has done …

If you really want to harm someone, one of the most effective means of doing so is to betray them. More insidious than physical injuries is denigration of self worth and the breaking down of the ability to trust anyone else. Many survivors engage in some form of mutilation or self harm, some even attempting suicide. On a summer's day when I see sets of faint scar lines on the bare arms of women I meet, I often wonder whether these are the scars of someone who has experienced some form of abuse. Others of us learnt to mutilate ourselves without a knife. Rather we came to believe the mantras which we said to ourselves repeatedly such as 'I'm a dreadful person', 'No one can love me', 'I deserved this' or variations on these themes.

What makes me really angry is when I hear self-mutilators denigrated as 'just being attention-seekers'. Usually only someone who is experiencing a hurt as deep as the hurt of betrayal will mutilate themselves and the compassion of Jesus is what is needed. Too bad that the betrayers have seemingly co-opted Jesus and the church to stand beside and give assent to their actions.

> Jesus
> Like you, I have been betrayed by those who I was supposed to be able to trust, who claimed that they loved and cared for me.
> The pain has at times left me utterly unconsolable, and unable to face life any longer.
> I know you don't condone what has happened to me, but sometimes it felt that even you didn't care.
> Breathe into me the strength and courage to want to embrace life, today, tomorrow and as long as it takes to recover from this profound betrayal.

43

LORD ANSWER ME

Wednesday Holy Week

> A religious person who is victimized by rape, battering, or child
> sexual abuse frequently faces the questions, Why do I suffer in this
> way? ... Where is God in my suffering? These profound theological
> questions cannot be answered simply with platitudes and then
> dismissed. The question of why there is suffering at all is one of
> classical theological debate ... to which there is no completely
> satisfactory answer. Human suffering in the midst of a world created
> by a compassionate and loving God is a dimension of human
> experience which is most disturbing and disquieting.

> —*Marie Fortune*

Psalm 69:16–21. *Why must I endure such degradation?*

UNFORTUNATELY, MOST PEOPLE ARE SUBJECTED to degrading
incidents at some point in their lives. Thankfully not everyone is
subjected to degradation on a par with rape or sexual abuse, but I'm not
sure I know anyone who has sailed through life escaping taunts and
insults which have left them feeling distressed and feeling desperately in
need of consolation. When consolation is not readily forthcoming, a
sense of abandonment can turn the despair from being a single
mountain which we need to conquer to an entire mountain range which
we somehow have to find a way of crossing, and which at this point feels
like a complete impossibility.

At times of utter despair, we understand how Jesus on the cross could
cry out 'My God, my God, why have you forsaken me?' The depth of

our pain might also have lead us to think that dying was our only release from our anguish, and irrespective of how we have responded to such thoughts, we may know others who have attempted, or even succeeded in, taking their own lives.

In some churches and Christian communities, people at the point of despair who find themselves crying out 'My God, my God, why have you forsaken me?' can find themselves feeling admonished for their 'lack of faith'. The admonishers seem to forget that Jesus himself cried out these words, and few would dare to say that he lacked faith.

When bad things happen and people cry out wondering where God is in the situation, maybe this doesn't mean they lack faith. Perhaps only the person who truly believes in God can cry 'My God, my God, why have you forsaken me?' Would those who have no faith utter this cry?

> Incomprehensible God
> Today we give thanks for those who cry out to you in utter despair, wanting to know why you have abandoned them.
> We give thanks for their fragile faith in which they still cling to the possibility that you exist and are part of their lives.
> And we pray they will find the comfort and consolation which they seek, rather than condemnation.

44

EUCHARIST

Maundy Thursday

> Eucharist is the liturgical realization of Christ's suffering and redemptive body on the bodies of his followers. Torture creates fearful and isolated bodies, bodies docile … the Eucharist effects the body of Christ, a body marked by resistance to worldly power. Torture creates victims; Eucharist creates witnesses, *martyrs.* Isolation is overcome in the Eucharist by the building of a communal body …

—*William Cavanaugh*

1 Corinthians 11:23–26. *The Lord's Supper*

THERE ARE SOME CHRISTIAN TRADITIONS in which the eucharist is rarely or never celebrated. There are others, particularly but not only the Catholic Church, where the celebration of eucharist occurs daily. Quite what lead me from the first to the second tradition and to my current life where I attend eucharist several days a week when that is possible, I'm not entirely sure. One could say that I had reached a point of despair and was experimenting with an alternate lifestyle in the search for happiness. However, perhaps I knew instinctively what it would take me years to be able to articulate.

A few years ago, I read William Cavanaugh's book about torture in which the author proposed that cruel violations of the body are an 'anti-liturgy'. If understood as an act of love which can promote healing, eucharist is a stark contrast to the cruelty which underlies violence. As such, eucharist becomes the 're-membering', or putting back together the broken body of Christ. Through this act, we too might find that it re-members our broken bodies and damaged souls. Hence, participation in liturgy and sacraments can be an antidote or part of the process of moving beyond abuse.

One of the ways in which this happened for me came with the realisation that whenever someone offered me the eucharistic elements, chances were that our fingers would brush past each other, touching ever so lightly. I recalled times when I would want to recoil from being touched by anyone, so the realisation that I could let strangers touch me and not be hurt felt like a revelation.

It is sometimes said that regular participation in organised worship, including eucharist, particularly for those for whom it is a daily part of their lives, may be a sign of weakness verging on 'religious addiction', although interestingly such claims only ever seem to be made about the laity and not those who become ordained clergy or members of recognised religious communities. However rather than being a sign of weakness, it could be argued that regular participation in the eucharist reflects a desire for life in the face of adversity.

> People sometimes wonder what's so important about a crumb of bread and a drop of wine,
> not enough to satisy a hunger or thirst of human proportions,
> yet, miraculously, these seemingly insignificant fragments make a difference,
> breathing hope into hopelessness,
> beckoning thankfulness.
>
> In remembrance of your life and death,
> we are reminded once again that the lowest points in our lives can be overcome,
> in the simple sharing of bread and wine.

45

CRUCIFIXION

Good Friday

> By identifying with Jesus the Crucified, one is able to name one's own victimization, to face the wounds that have hampered one's full human flourishing. ... the Crucified becomes friend instead of stranger, and resurrection is God's raising of one's belief in Self in the face of powerful messages to the contrary.

—Cynthia Crysdale

John 18:1–19:42. *Jesus' trial and death by crucifixion*

MANY SURVIVORS HAVE LIKENED THEIR experience of abuse to that of crucifixion; the painful image of Jesus on the cross is one with which they can strongly identify. As pain-bearer and life-giver, the crucified Christ, who loved the world so much that he was prepared to die for us, can be a profound symbol of hope for the oppressed.

Several works of art by prominent artists in recent decades have incorporated images of crucified women, and in doing so, have stirred up debate as to the desirability of such images. While many survivors have warmed to such images and reported a new-found affinity with the crucified Christ, opponents of female crucifixion imagery have been strident in their criticism. In the eyes of some, it is acceptable to re-image Jesus in many ways, as long as his gender is not altered. The appropriateness of survivors of abuse identifying with the crucified Jesus has been questioned by others. This is understandable, if, as some people mistakenly believe, identifying with the crucified Jesus includes enduring pain silently, as this may hinder the healing process.

Crucifixion is a horribly inhumane way of dying and not something that should in any way be glamorised or aspired to. Nevertheless, if contemplating Jesus on the cross provides a framework for making sense of the horror of the violation of one's very being, then it has a valid purpose.

Timothy Radcliffe tells the story of a Dominican named Brian Pierce, who went to the Peruvian Andes and wondered if the local people believed in the resurrection as many of the images of Christ were covered in blood. He subsequently learnt that these bloody crosses reflected an understanding that the risen Christ now shares in our crucifixion.

The following prayer was first written to mark the departure of a friend to live elsewhere. We had met a couple of years earlier when both of us had found ourselves in challenging situations, and for me at least, there had been a need to make sense of where God was. Looking back, it was clear that Christ had always been there, even when I felt most dejected and felt that I too had been crucified.

> When you were on the cross
> you were given no choice
> but to have your hands reach out
> to capture the hearts and minds of
> us who have found ourselves feeling
> lost
> confused
> confounded
> dejected
> in a place we did not want to be
> but somehow we believed you called us
> and although we sometimes wanted to run away
> the holy spirit breathed life into us
> helping us to grow

sometimes even to thrive
and just occasionally to feel enchanted.

46

COMMITMENT

Easter Vigil

I once gave an icon of Mary of Egypt to a woman who counsels teenage prostitutes. They range in age from ten—a girl who'd developed early, and whose stepfather and brothers have put her on the streets—to a world-weary eighteen. Many are runaways, most often from abusive homes, most have grown accustomed to being treated like trash. My friend's job is to convince them they aren't trash. She works hard—sometimes enduring threats from pimps—to help these girls see that they are good for something besides being bought and sold.

—*Kathleen Norris*

Romans 6:3–11. *Invitation to live a new life*

ONE OF THE MOST REMARKABLE features of the gospels is that Jesus calls a motley collection of people to follow him. Not only are the pasts of many of those called not pristine, but in many cases quite dubious. Somewhere on this continuum of characters called to follow Jesus there is space for those of us who have been subjected to the degradation and denigration of sexual abuse. In accepting this invitation, we may need to confront the fact that Jesus views us very much in the words of the writer of the Book of Wisdom who writes 'there is in her a spirit that is intelligent, holy, unique, manifold, subtle, mobile, clear, unpolluted, distinct, invulnerable, loving the good, keen, irresistible, beneficent, humane, steadfast, sure, free from anxiety, all-powerful, overseeing all, and penetrating through all spirits' (Wisdom 7:22b–23).

In some Christian traditions Easter is the time for baptism and welcoming new members into the church. But just as importantly, it is a time when all of us are invited to once again commit ourselves to the church and each other. As today's reading from Romans reminds us, our baptism was and is an invitation to live a new life. So as we renew our baptismal vows, we are symbolically reminded that a new life awaits us, irrespective of how terrible things have been in the past.

It's not always easy to takes the necessary steps forward to grasp a promised new life. Even if we're open to grasping that new life, there are challenges, with many options, some more life-giving than others. Do we want to swaddle ourselves in a hedonistic lifestyle, believing that we've earned the right for happiness at any cost after the suffering we've endured? Or do we choose to continue, however imperfectly, to commit ourselves to the teachings of Jesus.

Enabler God

As I renew my baptismal vows, help me to make choices that:

Enable me to make a contribution to your work in the world,

Enable me to be a pointer to your incarnation, and

Enable others to grow in their relationships with you.

47

RESURRECTION

Easter Sunday

… she said 'I didn't really think of myself as a *victim*. I didn't even think of myself as a *survivor* of abuse. And I still don't really. You see, *there's so much more to me than what they did to me*.' And she went on to talk about her life and work, and about her partner and the children they had together. She talked about the person she had become in that relationship. From a distance, if all I knew about her was the sickening details of what had been done to her, she would have appeared in every way to be a victim. But up close, in a personal meeting and the beginning of a friendship, she was recognizable as the interesting, accomplished, confident person that she is. The abuse, terrible as it was, was not the last word on her. What you do not see from a distance is the power at work in her which is 'on the side of life and fulfillment'.

—*Andrew Dutney*

Mark 16:1–8. *An empty tomb*

AN INDIVIDUAL'S DEATH FREQUENTLY MARKS the end of an era for a group or community. So it was for the women who visited the tomb with the expectation that they might pay a final act of love by anointing their beloved, and now dead, friend. Perhaps they were also wondering whether this was the end of what had been an amazing few years? What would become of them all? Would the group just drift apart, with people resuming the lives they were living before they all met Jesus? The possibility of resurrection, of a much better outcome than the finality of death, was not something that Mary of Magdala, Mary the mother of James, and Salome were contemplating as they made their way to the tomb.

With all the emphasis the church places on the death of Jesus and the period leading up to this, we too can feel unprepared for the resurrection. In today's reading from the gospel of Mark, after the lengthy account of all that occurred in the days leading up to and including Jesus' death, the story of his resurrection almost seems as if it is tacked on as a postscript.

In July 2006 I visited Dunedin and chanced upon a retrospective exhibition of New Zealand painter Michael Smither. One of his paintings, 'Crucifixion' has a face which is an empty shell. In the information displayed alongside this painting, Smither commented that the church has focused too much on the three days of Jesus' death and not enough on the resurrection, which he wanted to represent. This is the same challenge which confronts many survivors of abuse, namely, a belief that crucifixion will endure and that resurrection is eternally elusive. Sexual abuse doesn't have to be the final word. While what has happened can never be undone, eventually there may come a time when we feel able to enter a new phase of life and grasp the promise of resurrection.

It is finished,
and it is good,
and it is time to move on.

Loving God
Forgive me for my past wrongs
Guide me in my new beginnings
And sustain my faith when it all gets too much.

Thankfully amidst changes some things remain constant
    The body of Christ,
    The blood of Christ.

These signs of grace
    Beacons of forgiveness,
    Remind me that you are not yet finished,
    And won't cease from loving, caring for and forgiving me.

Notes

Introduction

This program of writing includes the following publications: Crisp, BR, 2001, 'Reading scripture from a hermeneutic of rape'. *Theology and Sexuality*, 14, pp. 23–42; Crisp, BR, 2004, 'Spiritual direction and survivors of sexual abuse'. *The Way*, 43 (2), pp. 7–17; Crisp, BR, 2007, Spirituality and sexual abuse: Issues and dilemmas for survivors'. *Theology and Sexuality*, 13, pp. 301–314; and Crisp, BR, 2009, 'Beyond crucifixion: Remaining Christian after sexual abuse'. *Theology and Sexuality*, 15, pp. 65–76.

1. Taking up the Challenge

Kathleen Norris, 1999, *The Cloister Walk*. Oxford: Lion Publishing, p. 19.

2. Rejection

Susan J Brison, 1993, 'Surviving sexual violence'. *Journal of Social Philosophy*, 24, p. 13.

3. The scandalised church

Marilyn Born, 2002, 'What Hollingworth should be saying', Letter to The Editor. *The Age* (Melbourne Australia) 26 February 2002, p. 14.

4. Conversion

Ann Ulanov and Barry Ulanov, 1982, *Primary Speech: A Psychology of Prayer*. Atlanta: John Knox Press, p. 10.

5. Seduction

Dorothy McRae-McMahon, 1998, *Everyday Passions: A Conversation on Living*. Sydney: ABC Books, p. 1.

6. Too hard

'Geraldine' in Helen Last, Mirta Gonzalez and Danny Valasz (eds), 1994, *Public Face Private Pain: The Anglican Report about Violence Against Women and the Abuse of Power within the Church Community*. Carlton, Victoria: CASA House, p. 27.

7. Fathers

'Helen' in Last et al. *Public Face Private Pain*, p. 27.

'Donna' in Joanne Ross Feldmeth and Midge Wallace Finley, 1990, *We Weep for Ourselves and Our Children: A Christian Guide for Survivors of Childhood Sexual Abuse*. New York: HarperSanFrancisco, p. 104.

8. Steadfast spirit

Gill Goulding, 2003, *Creative Perseverance: Sustaining Life-Giving Ministry in Today's Church*. Ottawa: Novalis, pp. 138–139.

Alice Sebold, 1990, 'Speaking of the unspeakable'. *Psychiatric Times*, 7, p. 34.

9. Suffering in silence

Craig Martin, 2002, 'Statement of Craig Martin Presented to the United States Conference of Catholic Bishops, 13 June 2002, Dallas Texas', http://www.usccb.org/bishops/martin.shtml, obtained 9 July 2006.

10. Confession

Paula Gonzales Rohrbacher, 2002, 'Impact Statement of Paula Gonzales Rorhbacher Presented to the United States Conference of Catholic Bishops, 13 June 2002, Dallas Texas', http://www.usccb.org/bishops/rohrbacher.shtml, obtained 9 July 2006.

11. Get real

Muriel Porter, 2003, *Sex, Power and the Clergy*. South Yarra, Victoria: Hardie Grant Books, p. 174.

12. Texts of terror

Tina Pippin, 1995, '"And I will strike her children dead": Death and the deconstruction of social location', in Fernando F Segovia and Mary Ann Tolbert (eds) *Readings from this Place Volume 1*. Minneapolis: Fortress Press, p. 198.

13. Low self esteem

Beth R Crisp, 2006, 'Ignatian spirituality and the rebuilding of self-esteem', *The Way*, 45(1), p. 66.

14. Wayward and bad
Carla van Raay, 2004, *God's Callgirl: A Memoir*. Sydney: HarperCollinsPublishers, p. 34.

15. Deliver me Lord
'Miriam' in Last et al. *Public Face Private Pain*, p. 76.

16. Blessings
Geoffrey Robinson, 2007, *Confronting Power and Sex in the Catholic Church: Reclaiming the Spirit of Jesus*. Mulgrave, Victoria: John Garrett Publishing, p. 217.

17. The favoured one
The words of her rapist as recalled by 'Sarah' in Derek Farrell and M Taylor, 2000, 'Silenced by God: An examination of unique characteristics within sexual abuse by clergy'. *Counselling Psychology Review*, 15(1), p. 24.

18. Spiritual direction
Lisa E Dahill, 2001, 'Reading from the underside of selfhood: Dietrich Bonhoeffer and spiritual formation'. *Spiritus*, 1, p. 194.

19. More texts of terror
Elly Danica, 1989, *Don't: A Woman's Word*. London: Womens Press, p. 15.

20. Thirsting for God
Diane R Garland, 2006, 'When wolves wear shepherds' clothing: Helping women survive clergy sexual abuse'. *Social Work and Christianity*, 33, p. 12.

21. Impossible demands
Misti Joy Woolery Lincoln, 2001, *A Balm in Gilead: The Role of the Church in Healing and Prevention of Child Sexual Abuse*. Master of Divinity dissertation, Emmanuel School of Religion, Johnson City Tennessee, p. 25.

22. According to God's plan?
Sandra Knauer, 2000, *Recovering from Sexual Abuse, Addictions and Compulsive Behaviors: 'Numb' Survivors*. New York: Haworth Social Work Practice Press, p.2.

23. Why doesn't a loving God prevent abuse?
Knauer, *Recovering from Sexual Abuse,* pp. 1–2.

24. Loving oneself
Dahill, 'Reading from the underside of selfhood', p. 192.

25. The need for healing
Rita E Guare, 2001, 'Educating in the ways of the spirit: Teaching and leading poetically, prophetically, powerfully'. *Religious Education*, 96, p. 74.

26. Consequences of breaking the silence
William T Cavanaugh, 1998, *Torture and Eucharist: Theology, Politics and the Body of Christ*. Malden MA: Blackwell Publishing, p. 43.

27. Mosaics
Robert Wuthnow, 2001, *Creative Spirituality: The Way of the Artist*. Berkeley: University of California Press, p. 75.

28. Spiritual direction
David L Fleming, 1996, *Draw Me Into Your Friendship: The Spiritual Exercises, A Literal Translation and a Contemporary Reading*. St Louis: Institute of Jesuit Sources, p. 9.

This prayer was originally published in Crisp, 'Ignatian spirituality and the rebuilding of self-esteem', pp. 69–70.

29 Timeframes
Timothy Radcliffe, 2005, *What is the Point of Being a Christian?* London: Burn & Oates, p. 78.

30. The need to be believed
Youtha C Hardman-Cromwell, 2005, 'Killing silence'. *Journal of Religious Thought*, 57/58 (2/1-2), p. 173.

31. The imperfect but loving God
Timothy Radcliffe, 2008, *Why Go to Church? The Drama of the Eucharist*. London: Continuum, p.16.

32. The long term effects of abuse
Patrick Parkinson, 1997, *Child Sexual Abuse and the Churches*. London: Hodder & Staughton, p. 112.

33. Survivors not victims

Radcliffe, *What is the Point of Being a Christian?* p. 36.

34. Put on trial

Susan Estrich, 1987, *Real Rape*. Cambridge, Ma: Harvard University Press, p. 2.

35. Remembering to be thankful

Rachel Lev, 2003, *Shine the Light: Sexual Abuse and Healing in the Jewish Community*. Boston: Northeastern University Press, p. 135.

36. Miraculous survival

Laurel Lewis, 1995, 'Growing beyond abuse', in John C Gonsoriek (ed), *Breach of Trust: Sexual Exploitation by Health Care Professionals and Clergy*. Thousand Oaks: Sage, p. 49.

37. No longer believe in God

Lev, *Shine the Light*, p. xxvii.

38. A time for giving thanks

Joanna Gilbert, 2008, 'One step enough for me', in Laurentia Johns (ed), *Touched by God: Ten Monastic Journeys*. London: Burns & Oates, p. 11.

39. This is the word of the Lord?

Danna Nolan Fewell, 1997, 'Imagination, method and murder: Un/framing the face of post-exilic Israel', in Timothy K Beal and David M Gunn (eds), *Reading Bibles, Writing Bodies: Identity and the Book*. London: Routledge, p. 145.

40. On a journey

Mark Barrett, 2007, *Crossing: Reclaiming the Landscape of Our Lives*, new edition. London: DLT, p. 30.

41. Anointing

Lev, *Shine the Light*, p. 82.

42. Suffering in silence

Robinson, *Confronting Power and Sex in the Catholic Church*, p. 217.

43. Lord answer me

Marie F Fortune, 1989, 'The transformation of suffering: A biblical and theological perspective', in Joanne C Brown and Carole R Bohn (eds), *Christianity, Patriarchy and Abuse: A Feminist Critique*. New York: The Pilgrim Press, p. 139.

44. Eucharist

Cavanaugh, *Torture and Eucharist*, p. 206.

45. Crucifixion

Cynthia SW Crysdale, 1999, *Embracing Travail: Retrieving the Cross Today*. New York: Continuum, p. 10.

Radcliffe, *What is the Point of Being a Christian?* p. 75.

This prayer was originally published as 'Prayer to the Crucified One' in Crisp, 'Ignatian spirituality and the rebuilding of self-esteem', p. 72.

46. Commitment

Norris, *The Cloister Walk*, p. 181.

47. Resurrection

Andrew Dutney, 2005, 'Hoping for the best: Christian theology of hope in the meaner Australia', in JA Eliott (ed), *Interdisciplinary Perspectives on Hope*. New York: Nova Science Publishers, p. 57.

Works cited

Barrett, M, 2007, *Crossing: Reclaiming the Landscape of Our Lives*, new edition. London: DLT.

Born, M, 2002, 'What Hollingworth should be saying'. Letter to the Editor, *The Age* (Melbourne Australia) 26 February 2002, p. 14.

Brison, SJ, 1993, 'Surviving sexual violence'. *Journal of Social Philosophy*, 24, pp. 5–22.

Cavanaugh, WT, 1998, *Torture and Eucharist: Theology, Politics and the Body of Christ*. Malden MA: Blackwell Publishing.

Crisp, BR, 2006, 'Ignatian spirituality and the rebuilding of self-esteem'. *The Way*, 45(1), pp. 66–78.

Crysdale, CSW, 1999, *Embracing Travail: Retrieving the Cross Today*. New York: Continuum.

Dahill, LE, 2001 'Reading from the underside of selfhood: Dietrich Bonhoeffer and spiritual formation'. *Spiritus*, 1, pp. 186–203.

Danica, E, 1989, *Don't: A Woman's Word*. London: Womens Press.

Dutney, A, 2005, 'Hoping for the best: Christian theology of hope in the meaner Australia', in JA Eliott (ed), *Interdisciplinary Perspectives on Hope*, New York: Nova Science Publishers.

Estrich, S, 1987, *Real Rape*. Cambridge, Ma: Harvard University Press.

Farrell, D and Taylor, M, 2000, 'Silenced by God: An examination of unique characteristics within sexual abuse by clergy'. *Counselling Psychology Review*, 15(1), pp. 22–31.

Feldmeth, JR and Finley, MW, 1990, *We Weep for Ourselves and Our Children: A Christian Guide for Survivors of Childhood Sexual Abuse*. New York: HarperSanFrancisco.

Fewell, DN, 1997, 'Imagination, method and murder: Un/framing the face of post-exilic Israel', in TK Beal and DM Gunn (eds), *Reading Bibles, Writing Bodies: Identity and the Book*. London: Routledge.

Fleming, DL, 1996, *Draw Me Into Your Friendship: The Spiritual Exercises, A Literal Translation and a Contemporary Reading*, St Louis: Institute of Jesuit Sources.

Fortune, MF, 1989 'The transformation of suffering: A biblical and theological perspective', in JC Brown and CR Bohn (eds), *Christianity, Patriarchy and Abuse: A Feminist Critique*. New York: The Pilgrim Press.

Garland, DR, 2006, 'When wolves wear shepherds' clothing: Helping women survive clergy sexual abuse'. *Social Work and Christianity*, 33, pp 1–35.

Gilbert, J, 2008, 'One step enough for me', in L Johns (ed), *Touched by God: Ten Monastic Journeys*. London: Burns & Oates.

Goulding, G, 2003 *Creative Perseverance: Sustaining Life-Giving Ministry in Today's Church*. Ottawa: Novalis.

Guare, RE, 2001, 'Educating in the ways of the spirit: Teaching and leading poetically, prophetically, powerfully'. *Religious Education*, 96, pp. 65–87.

Hardman-Cromwell, YC, 2005, 'Killing silence', *Journal of Religious Thought* 57/58 (2/1-2), pp. 169–179.

Knauer, S, 2000, *Recovering from Sexual Abuse, Addictions and Compulsive Behaviors: 'Numb' Survivors*. New York: Haworth Social Work Practice Press.

Last, H, Gonzalez, M and Valasz, D (eds), 1994, *Public Face Private Pain: The Anglican Report about Violence Against Women and the Abuse of Power within the Church Community*. Carlton, Victoria: CASA House.

Lev, R, 2003, *Shine the Light: Sexual Abuse and Healing in the Jewish Community*. Boston: Northeastern University Press.

Lewis, L, 1995, 'Growing beyond abuse', in JC Gonsoriek (ed), *Breach of Trust: Sexual Exploitation by Health Care Professionals and Clergy*, Thousand Oaks: Sage.

Lincoln, MJW, 2001, *A Balm in Gilead: The Role of the Church in Healing and Prevention of Child Sexual Abuse*, Master of Divinity dissertation, Emmanuel School of Religion, Johnson City Tennessee.

McRae-McMahon, D, 1998, *Everyday Passions: A Conversation on Living*, Sydney: ABC Books.

Martin, C, 2002, 'Statement of Craig Martin Presented to the United States Conference of Catholic Bishops, 13 June 2002, Dallas Texas', http://www.usccb.org/bishops/martin.shtml, obtained 9 July 2006.

Norris, K, 1999, *The Cloister Walk*. Oxford: Lion Publishing.

Parkinson, P, 1997, *Child Sexual Abuse and the Churches*. London: Hodder & Staughton.

Pippin, T, 1995 '"And I will strike her children dead": Death and the deconstruction of social location', in FF Segovia and MA Tolbert (eds), *Readings from this Place Volume 1*. Minneapolis: Fortress Press.

Porter, M, 2003, *Sex, Power and the Clergy*. South Yarra, Victoria: Hardie Grant Books.

Radcliffe, T, 2005, *What is the Point of Being a Christian?* London: Burn & Oates.

Radcliffe, T, 2008, *Why Go to Church? The Drama of the Eucharist*. London: Continuum.

Robinson, G, 2007, *Confronting Power and Sex in the Catholic Church: Reclaiming the Spirit of Jesus*. Mulgrave, Victoria: John Garrett Publishing.

Rohrbacher, PG, 2002, 'Impact Statement of Paula Gonzales Rohrbacher Presented to the United States Conference of Catholic Bishops, 13 June 2002, Dallas Texas', http://www.usccb.org/bishops/rohrbacher.shtml, obtained 9 July 2006.

Sebold, A, 1990, 'Speaking of the unspeakable', *Psychiatric Times*, 7, pp. 34–35.

van Raay, C, 2004, *God's Callgirl: A Memoir*. Sydney: HarperCollinsPublishers.

Ulanov, A and Ulanov, B, 1982 *Primary Speech: A Psychology of Prayer*. Atlanta: John Knox Press.

Wuthnow, R, 2001, *Creative Spirituality: The Way of the Artist*. Berkeley: University of California Press.